Kaffe Fassett's
Caravan of Quilts

Patchwork and Quilting
book number 6

Kaffe Fassett • Brandon Mably • Pauline Smith • Sandy Donabed • Betsy Mennesson
Liza Prior Lucy • Mary Mashuta • Roberta Horton • Gill Turley

A ROWAN PUBLICATION

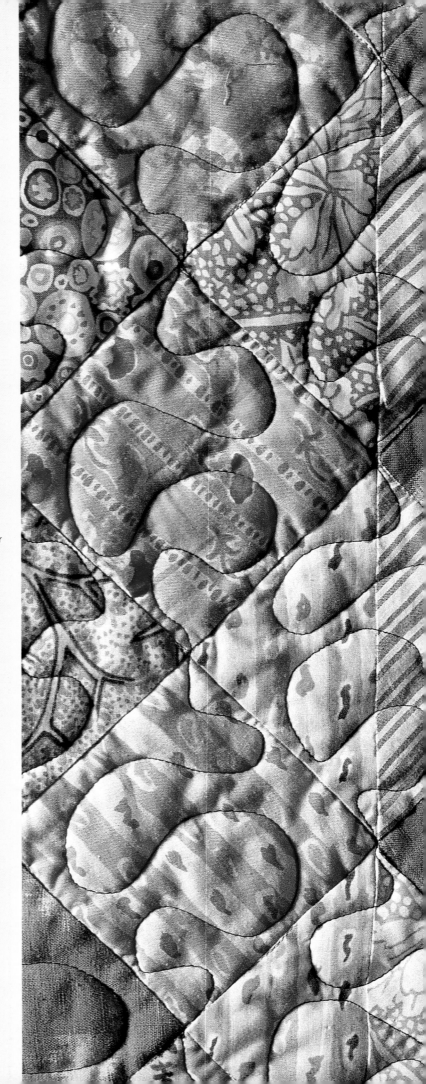

First Published in Great Britain in 2004 by
Rowan Yarns
Green Lane Mill
Holmfirth
West Yorkshire
England
HD9 2DX

Art Director: Kaffe Fassett
Technical editors: Ruth Eglinton and Pauline Smith
Co-ordinator: Pauline Smith
Editorial Director: Kate Buller
Patchwork Designs: Kaffe Fassett, Liza Prior Lucy, Pauline
                         Smith, Roberta Horton, Mary Mashuta,
                         Gill Turley, Brandon Mably, Sandy
                         Donabed and Betsy Mennesson.

Quilters: Judy Irish, Terry Clark
Sewer   Janet Stoner
Photography: Debbie Patterson
Flat shot photography: DaveTolson @ Visage

Styling: Kaffe Fassett
Design Layout: Christine Wood - Gallery of Quilts/
                                           front section
                         Simon Wagstaff - instructions &
                                          technical information
Illustrations: Ruth Eglinton
Feature: Susan Berry
Photography   Mike Smith pages 6 - 7

British Library Cataloguing in Publication Data
Rowan Yarns
Patchwork and Quilting
ISBN 1-904485-23-5

Colour reproduction by Chroma Graphics (Overseas) Pte. Ltd
Printed and bound in Singapore by KHL. Printing Co. Pte. Ltd

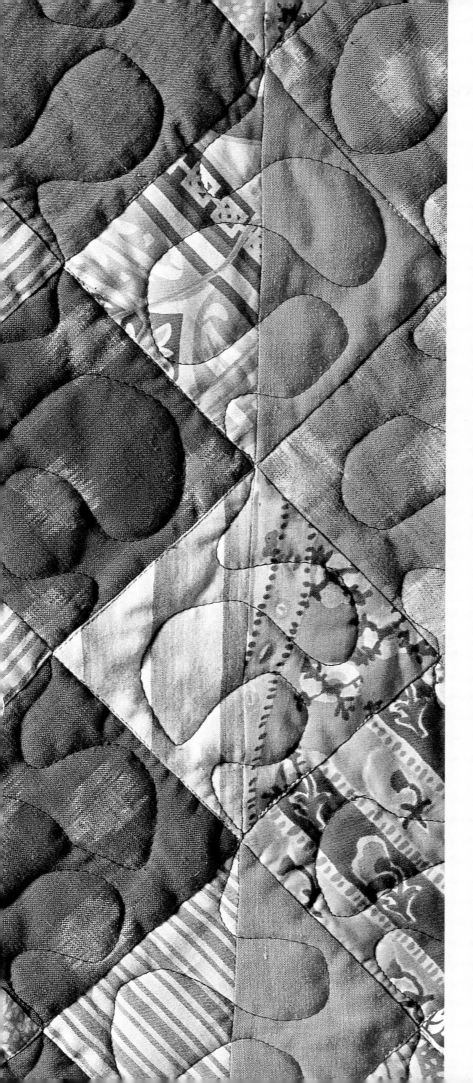

contents

introduction

Most people know that I am interested in low-contrast colour harmonies, but for those who do not, I should explain that I get a sense of drama in my quilt designs from building up pools of colour rather than from startling dark and light contrasts. Therefore, I like to use fabrics that are very similar in texture and colour to create quilt designs that employ similarly subtle changes. The collection of fabrics that I have designed for Rowan, which form the basis for the quilts in this book, and are shown on pages 115 to 121, allow me to explore these values.

The title of this new book, *Caravan of Quilts* - the sixth in the Rowan series -sprang from a gorgeous set of old gypsy caravans that we found in the English New Forest. Gypsy caravans are renowned for their wonderfully rich and patterned decoration. I think this mirrors the art of the quilt maker, so they provided us with a wonderful background against which to photograph some of the quilts in this book, in particular the *Wheel of Fortune* quilt on the cover and the *Gilded Frames* floor cushion project on page 1.

To continue the theme of pattern on pattern, we shot the remainder of the quilts at the house of a friend, who is as enthusiastic a collector of decorative arts as I am. As you can see in the shots of many of the quilts he has painted his house, a former Victorian vicarage, in the most wonderful, off-the-wall, palette of colours. The rich and varied background, and the wonderfully eclectic artefacts, turned out to be the ideal choice to echo the different moods of the quilts in this book.

Caravan of Quilts, as with the previous books in the series, showcases the work of a group of designers as well as my own. I am very glad to be able to introduce some new names to the group of those who already design quilts in the series.

To the original group of Liza Prior Lucy, Pauline Smith, Mary Mashuta, Roberta Horton, Sandy Donabed and Brandon Mably - all of whose work always delights - we have added a couple of interesting new designers, each contributing their own particular style and colour choices. It is nice to include the fresh colours from Oregon of Betsy Mennesson. I should point out that Betsy's quilts also have a secondary appeal: the reverse side is made up of a patchwork of shot cotton which is particularly attractive (a detail of this can be seen on page 15). I do think the back of a quilt should relate in some way, even if by contrast, to the front of the quilt. In addition to Betsy's work, we also have the subtle colour palettes of Gill Turley from England.

Kaffe Fassett

Whimsical Basket by Betsy Menneson
Several shades of shot cottons show the clever quilting on the back of Betsy's quilt.

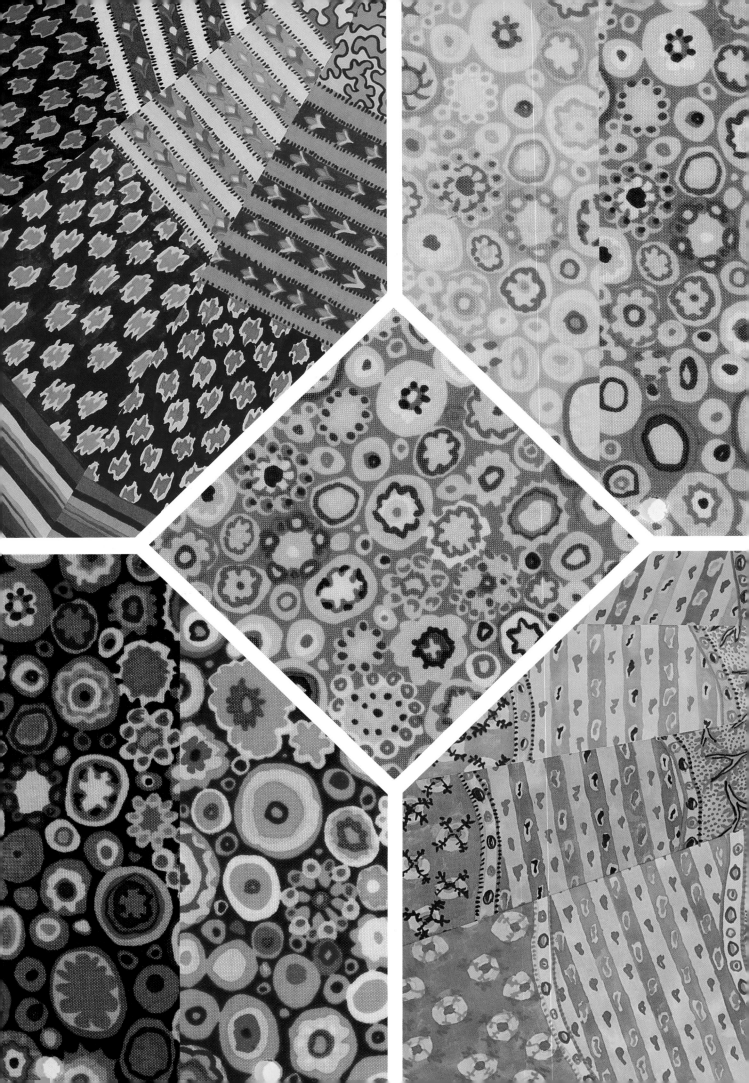

the fabrics

Each season we add a collection of new fabrics to the existing range (see pages 115 - 121), and each collection has its own unique design source. The fabrics are woven in India and I find sourcing them a thrilling experience. It is a delight to go to a country that is obsessed with textiles and where they still create extraordinary weaving and wonderful embroidery of every type, texture and colouring.

I sit sometimes for four or five days, going through archives dating back for decades. From these I pick out various ideas that catch my eye - perhaps the corner of a fabric which might translate into an entirely new and modern design.

Other ideas can spark off a new collection, as well as build on the existing designs. One new set of fabrics, such as the Ikat stripes, based on the famous traditional dyeing technique, has inspired in its turn a totally new kind of stripe that I shall be adding next season.

Our printed range is manufactured in Japan and Korea. One of the driving inspirations for the new prints in my range this year is a flirtation I'm having with antique quilts at the Victoria and Albert Museum, London. I am currently working on a book that will portray my version of some of the old English quilts in the museum. When you look at them carefully you see that a lot of the fabrics are extremely simple two or three colour designs that read well, singing out in the melange of patterns.

As it is difficult for me to design a very simple fabric and launch it in the market I have combined four simple ideas in each of two new fabric designs - one is called Organic Stripe the other is called Swiggle Stripe. These have been created in various colourways. It never fails to surprise me how much mileage one can get out of each of these fabrics.

The best example of this in our new collection is the *Big Bang* quilt - see page 20-21. It uses five colourways of these two fabrics, plus just two other prints, for the entire quilt. When you glance across the surface it looks like at least twenty different fabrics!

The other textiles in the current collection that I developed in India are Double Ikats. These are very graphic ideas that make a crisp profile. Polka is a simple dot motif and the other is a two colour check called Checkerboard. They are constructed of a two colour dyed weft woven on a two colour warp. Getting the design to join up is a very exacting and time consuming process that can only be done by hand. The result has a rustic charm that is exactly what I was after. When we were in India researching this collection we visited the village that specialised in this ancient craft and watched the dyers tie dyeing the warps and wefts. For close ups in a quilt see pages 10 - 11 as both fabrics are used in Roberta Horton's *Tree of Life*.

The third group of fabrics being launched is Pansies, Kashmir, and Paper Weight - which was inspired by a paperweight I saw in Liza Prior Lucy's house. It is similar in design to the very popular Roman Glass but a little more intricate. I have a great fondness for dotty, spotty fabrics which seems to find an enthusiasm amongst my fans. These three new designs are small scale, intricately detailed, fabrics that will work well with previous patterns like Roman Glass and Peony.

I hope that you have as much pleasure in creating these quilts as we did designing and making them and that you find our new fabrics a source of future inspiration.

Beaded Curtain - Kaffe Fassett
Shown here on a wall of Candace Bahouth's Mosaic Studio.

Tree of Life by Roberta Horton
The bed side vase reflects the geometry of Roberta Horton's *Tree of Life* quilt.

Sophisticated Play by Mary Mashuta
Mary's quilt is echoed elegantly by the rich collection of pottery.

Whimsical Basket by Betsy Mennesson
The unexpected wall colours and collection of porcelain figurines make a beautiful setting for Betsy's *Whimsical Basket*.

Canyon Star by Kaffe Fassett
Shades of terracotta on this terrace set off Kaffe's *Canyon Star* quilt.

Big Diamond quilt by Kaffe Fassett and Pauline Smith's *Zig Zag* bag relate well to this old Japanese marquetry.

Big Bang by Kaffe Fassett
Kaffe's *Big Bang* quilt explodes in this English Garden Court.

Pastel Gridlock by Liza Prior Lucy
Pastel Gridlock makes a delicate curtain for this garden pergola.

24

Cinque De Mayo by Sandy Donabed
The Victorian tiles and orange pots compliment *Cinque De Mayo* quilt by Sandy Donabed.

Wheel Of Fortune by Kaffe Fassett
The bold colours of the *Wheel of Fortune* are set off by the deep tones of this gypsy caravan.

Rippled Diamonds by Brandon Mably
Brandon's soothing *Rippled Diamonds* quilt glows in this pink door way. (also on back cover)

Heather Strippy quilt by Gill Turley
Gill's *Heather Strippy* quilt looks handsome in this Victorian setting.

Sky Blue Pink by Kaffe Fassett
This decaying camellia bush is a perfect companion for *Sky Blue Pink* quilt.

Monkey Puzzle by Pauline Smith
This wicker ware goose basket echoes the colours and form of Pauline's *Monkey Puzzle* bed cover.

Gilded Frames Floor Cushion by Kaffe Fassett and *Soft Boxes* by
Liza Prior Lucy glow in this deep Victorian colour pallette.

Ebay On Point by Kaffe Fassett
Looks jaunty against this collection of Cornishware pottery.

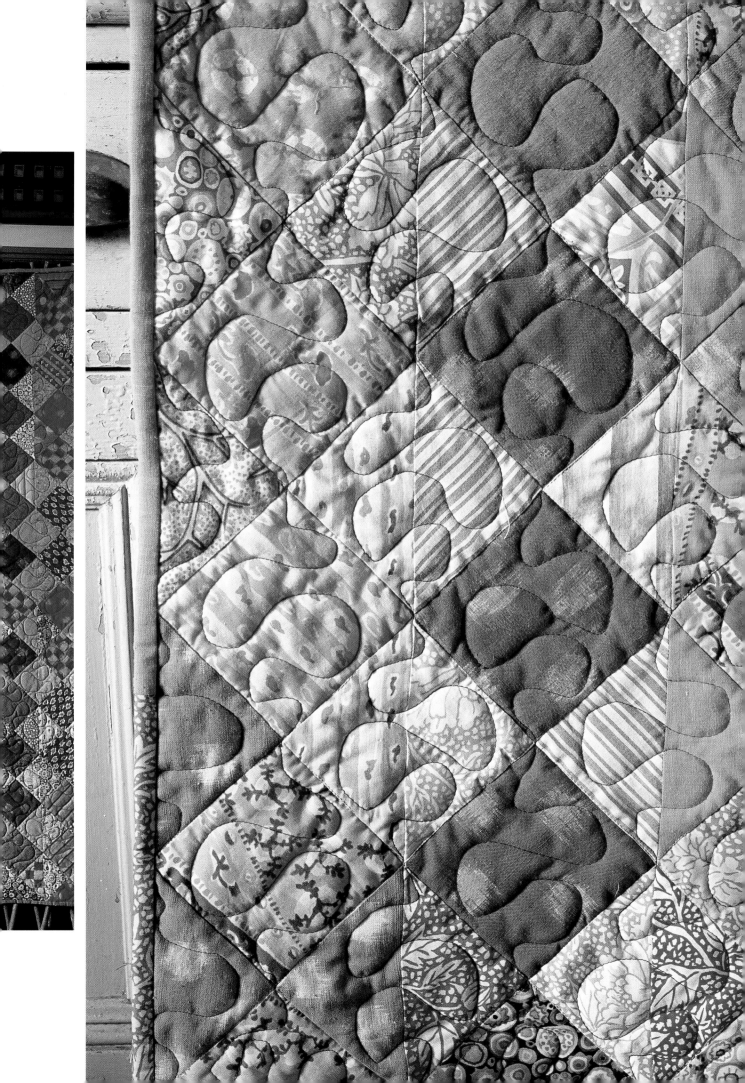

Hot Sauce Quilt by Liza Prior Lucy
Liza's quilt looks exciting in this Victorian
window setting.

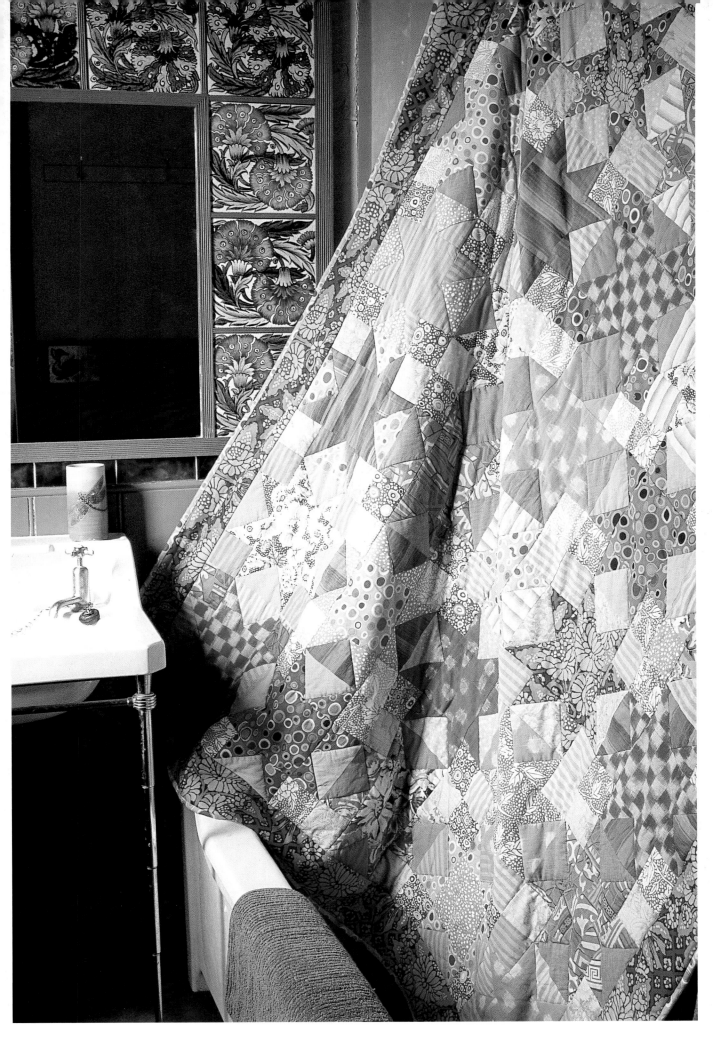

Blue Star by Kaffe Fassett
Kaffe's *Blue Star* quilt hanging against the rich blue tiles.

Gilded Frames Floor Cushion ★ ★ ★

KAFFE FASSETT

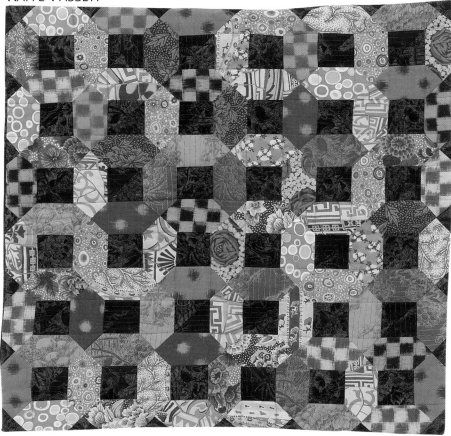

The ochre and golds in this design looked like gilded frames around small, dark pictures.

SIZE OF CUSHION
The finished cushion will measure approx. 34in x 34in (86.5cm x 86.5cm).

MATERIALS
Patchwork Fabrics:

ROMAN GLASS
Gold	GP01-G:	¹/₄yd (25cm)

DAMASK
Jewel	GP02-J:	¹/₈yd (15cm)
Plum Gold	GP02-PG:	¹/₈yd (15cm)

FORGET-ME-NOT ROSE
Jewel	GP08-J:	¹/₈yd (15cm)

BUBBLES
Ochre	GP15-O:	¹/₈yd (15cm)

MOSAIC
Red Gold	GP16-RG:	¹/₄yd (25cm)

PEONY
Maroon	GP17-MR:	¹/₈yd (15cm)

FRIUT BASKET
Black	GP19-BK:	1¹/₂yds (1.4m)
Gold	GP19-GD:	¹/₈yd (15cm)
Red	GP19-RD:	¹/₈yd (15cm)
Teal	GP19-TE:	¹/₈yd (15cm)

ORGANIC STRIPE
Brown	GP21-BR:	¹/₄yd (25cm)

DOUBLE IKAT CHECKERBOARD
Scarlet	DiC 01:	¹/₈yd (15cm)
Indigo	DiC 03:	¹/₈yd (15cm)
Gold	DiC 04:	¹/₈yd (15cm)

DOUBLE IKAT POLKA
Pumpkin	DiP 02:	¹/₈yd (15cm)
Scarlet	DiP 03:	¹/₈yd (15cm)

Lining Fabric:
Muslin or calico
36in x 36in (91cm x 91cm).

Batting:
36in x 36in (91cm x 91cm).

Quilting thread:
Toning machine quilting thread.

Templates:
see pages 102, 104, 106

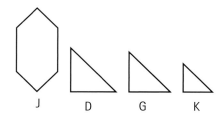

PATCH SHAPES
This floor cushion is made using one lozenge patch shape (Template J) and three triangle patch shapes (Templates D, G and K). These are pieced into diagonal rows using the 'inset seams' method. Using the black fabric gives the illusion of squares within frames, when in fact the shapes are triangles.

CUTTING OUT
Template J: Cut 3in (7.75cm) wide strips across the width of the fabric. Each strip will give you 7 patches per 45in (114cm) wide fabric. Cut 10 in GP16-RG, 9 in GP21-BR, 8 in GP01-G, 6 in GP19-GD, 5 in GP02-J, GP15-O, GP19-TE, DiC 01, DiC 03, DiP 02, 4 in GP17-MR, GP19-RD, DiP 03, 3 in GP02-PG, GP08-J and DiC 04.
Template D: Cut 3⁵/₈in (9.25cm) wide strips across the width of the fabric. Each strip will give you 24 patches per 45in (114cm) wide fabric. Cut 72 in GP19-BK.
Template G: Cut one 3³/₈in (8.5cm) wide strip across the width of the fabric. Cut 4 in GP19-BK. Reserve the remaining fabric strip to cut template K.
Template K: Using the reserved strip from template G, trim the strip to 2³/₈in (6cm) wide and cut 20 in GP19-BK.

Cushion Reverse: Cut 2 pieces 22in x 34¹/₂in (56cm x 87.5cm) in GP19-BK.

MAKING THE CUSHION FRONT
Lay out all the patch shapes in the correct combination to form the cushion front, referring to the cushion assembly diagram for fabric placement. Separate the diagonal rows carefully. Using a ¹/₄in (6mm) seam allowance throughout, stitch the template J shapes together, see example row diagram a. Then inset the

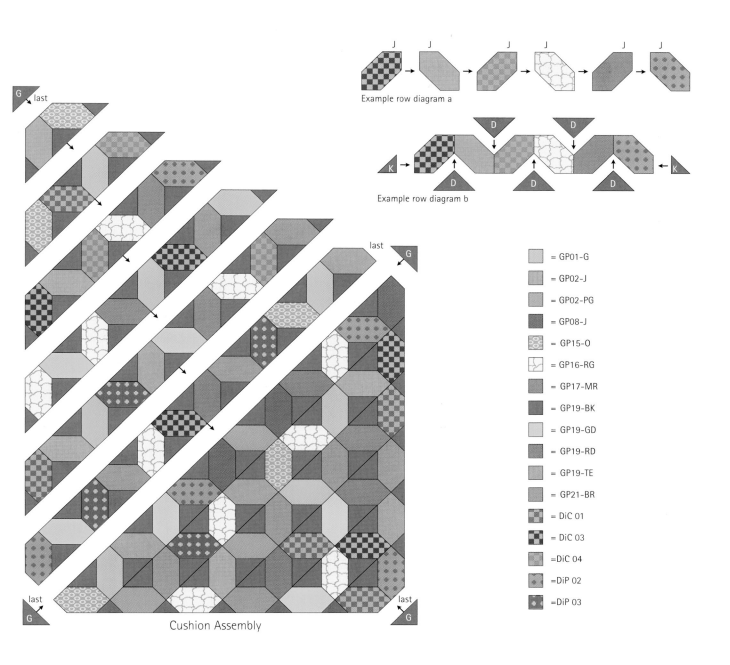

Example row diagram a

Example row diagram b

Cushion Assembly

= GP01-G
= GP02-J
= GP02-PG
= GP08-J
= GP15-O
= GP16-RG
= GP17-MR
= GP19-BK
= GP19-GD
= GP19-RD
= GP19-TE
= GP21-BR
= DiC 01
= DiC 03
=DiC 04
=DiP 02
=DiP 03

template D shapes into the row using the inset seams method (see page 110), see example row diagram b, then add the template K shapes to the ends of the rows where indicated (the 2 centre rows do not have these added). Assemble the diagonal rows and finally add the corner triangles, template G.

MAKING THE CUSHION REVERSE
Take the two cushion reverse pieces in GP19-BK, press a double ¹/₂in (1.5cm) hem to the wrong side of one long edge of each piece and stitch in place, close to the first pressed edge.

FINISHING THE CUSHION
Press the cushion front, layer with the batting and lining and baste together. Machine quilt a simple 'square' design as indicated on the cushion assembly diagram. Trim the batting and lining to match the cushion front. Place the cushion front right sides together with the two back pieces, overlapping the backs in the centre to form an envelope effect. Stitch the cushion front to the backs all around the edge. Trim back any excess batting in the seam to reduce bulk, turn the cushion through and insert pad through the envelope style back.

Quilting Diagram

Tree Of Life Quilt ★ ★

Roberta Horton

Roberta has created a contemporary version of the traditional Tree of Life pattern using the Double Ikat Checkerboard fabric. The polka dots provide a perfect finishing touch to this very graphic quilt.

SIZE OF QUILT
The finished quilt will measure approx.
59¹/₂in x 71¹/₂in (151cm x 181.5cm).

MATERIALS
Patchwork Fabrics:
Note: The quantity of fabric quoted for DiP 03 is generous, this allows the borders to be cut from the length of the fabric and avoids fiddly joining and matching of the dots. If you wish to be a little more economical and join the borders, buy 1 yd (90cm).
DIAGONAL POPPY
Lavender   GP24-LV: 1¹/₃yds (1.25m)

DOUBLE IKAT CHECKERBOARD
Indigo   DiC 03: 1 yd (90cm)
DOUBLE IKAT POLKA
Scarlet   DiP 03: 1⁷/₈ yds (1.7m)
avoids joins in the border.
SHOT COTTON
Tangerine   SC 11: ³/₈ yd (35cm)
Grape   SC 47: ³/₈ yd (35cm)
Mist   SC 48: ⁷/₈ yd (80cm)
Backing Fabric:
DIAGONAL POPPY
Aubergine   GP24-AU: 3⁵/₈ yds (3.3m)
Binding Fabric:
SHOT COTTON
Lichen   SC 19: ¹/₂ yd (45cm)

Batting:
64in x 76in (162.5cm x 193cm).
Quilting thread:
Maroon and Dark Gold machine quilting thread.

Templates:
see pages 99, 100, 105, 107

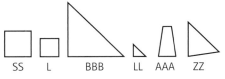

PATCH SHAPES
The quilt centre is made from blocks pieced using 3 triangle patch shapes (Templates LL, ZZ and BBB) and 1 lozenge patch shape (Template AAA). The blocks are interspaced with sashing cut to size and corner posts (Template L) and then surrounded with a bold border also with corner posts (Template SS). You'll find half template BBB on page 107. Take a large piece of paper, fold, place edge of template BBB to fold of paper, trace around shape and cut out. Open out for the complete template. Trace the completed shape into template plastic and mark on the seam line (this makes fussy cutting easy).

CUTTING OUT
Note: The fabric that Roberta chose for block background is reversible, however if you choose non reversible fabrics you will need to make an additional 'reverse' template for Shape ZZ.
Template L: Cut 3¹/₂in (9cm) wide strips across the width of the fabric. Each strip will give you 12 patches per 45in (114cm) wide fabric. Cut 30 in SC 11.
Template LL: Cut 2⁷/₈in (7.25cm) wide strips across the width of the fabric. Each strip will give you 28 patches per 45in (114cm) wide fabric. Cut 20 in SC 48.
Template SS: Cut 4³/₄in (12cm) wide strips. Cut 4 in SC 47.
Template ZZ: Cut 4⁵/₈in (11.75cm) wide strips across the width of the fabric. Each strip will give you 9 patches per 45in (114cm) wide fabric. Cut 40 in SC 48.

Quilt Assembly

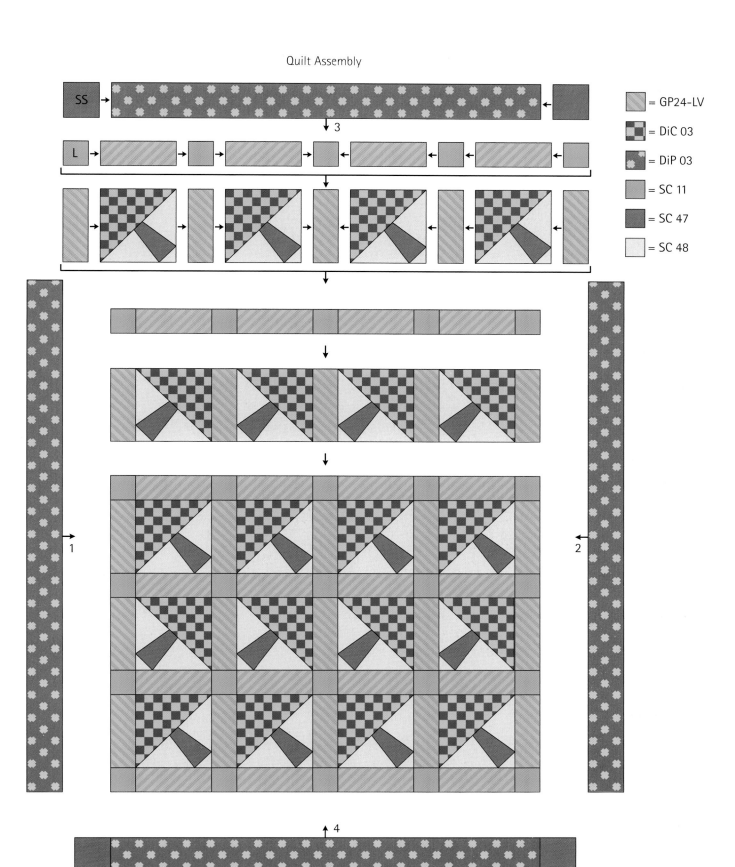

= GP24-LV

= DiC 03

= DiP 03

= SC 11

= SC 47

= SC 48

Template AAA: Cut 5¹/₂in (14cm) wide strips across the width of the fabric. Each strip will give you 16 patches per 45in (114cm) wide fabric. Cut 20 in SC 47.

Template BBB: These patch shapes are fussy cut. Position the template on the fabric so that the dark square in the fabric pattern is in the right angle corner of the template, aligning the square with the seam line (not the cutting line). The woven fabric is pliable and can be pulled into the correct alignment with the template.
Mark and cut the triangle. Don't worry if the cut triangle is a little misshapen, the sashing is cut on the straight grain which will keep the block in proper alignment. Cut each triangle individually to keep the patterning consistent. Cut 20 in DiC 03.

Sashing: Cut 3¹/₂in (9cm) wide strips across the width of the fabric. Each strip will give you 4 patches per 45in (114cm) wide fabric. Cut 49 strips 3¹/₂in x 9¹/₂in (9cm x 24.75cm) in GP24-LV.

Borders: Cut 2 strips 4³/₄in x 63¹/₂in (12cm x 161.25cm) and 2 strips 4³/₄in x 51¹/₂in (12cm x 131cm) down the length of the fabric in DiP 03. Cutting the borders this way avoids fiddly matching of the polka dots.

Backing: Cut 1 piece 64in x 45in (162.5cm x 114cm), and 1 piece 32in x 64in (81cm x 162.5cm) in GP24-AU.

Binding: Cut 7 strips 2¹/₂in (6.5cm) wide strips across the width of the fabric in SC 19.

MAKING THE BLOCKS
Using a ¹/₄in (6mm) seam allowance throughout, make up 20 blocks, using the block assembly diagram as a guide.

MAKING THE ROWS
Arrange the blocks and sashing pieces into rows as indicated in the quilt assembly diagram. Join the rows to form the quilt centre.

ADDING THE BORDERS
Add the corner posts to the ends of the top and bottom borders, then add the borders to the quilt centre in the order indicated by the quilt assembly diagram.

FINISHING THE QUILT
Press the quilt top. Seam the backing pieces using a ¹/₄in (6mm) seam allowance to form a piece approx. 64in x 76in (162.5cm x 193cm). Layer the quilt top, batting and backing and baste together (see page 112). Machine quilt as indicated in the quilting diagram, using invisible thread for the sashing seams. Black quilting thread is used for the checkerboard tree, following the fabric design. Purple quilting thread is used on the sashing, again following the design of the fabric, quilting every 2nd stripe. Light blue quilting thread is used for a loose meandering pattern in the tree block background. This colour is also used for the diagonal lines indicated in blue on the quilting diagram. Finally red quilting thread is used for parallel lines in the borders. Trim the quilt edges and attach the binding (see page 113).

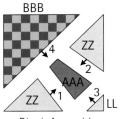

Block Assembly

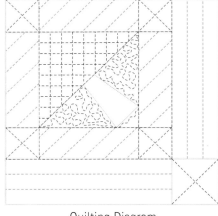

Quilting Diagram

Big Bang Quilt ★ ★ ★

Kaffe Fassett

I have always loved these huge explosions of diamonds like a Texas Star without borders. My new fabrics lend themselves so well to the blending that makes this happen.

SIZE OF QUILT
The finished quilt will measure approx. 95in x 95in (241cm x 241cm).

MATERIALS
Patchwork Fabrics:
DAMASK
Jewel   GP02-J: 5/8yd (60cm)
Plum Gold   GP02-PG: 3/4yd (70cm)
              or use leftover
              from backing.
Sage   GP02-SA: 1yd (90cm)
PAPERWEIGHT
Sludge   GP20-SL: 7/8yd (80cm)
ORGANIC STRIPE
Blue   GP21-BL: 2 1/4yds (2.1m)
Brown   GP21-BR: 3 3/4yds (3.4m)
Green   GP21-GN: 2 3/4yds (2.5m)
SWIGGLE
Green   GP22-GN: 1 1/4yds (1.15m)
Ochre   GP22-OC: 3 3/4yds (3.4m)

Backing Fabric:
DAMASK
Plum Gold   GP02-PG: 8 1/2yds (7.8m)
Binding Fabric:
DAMASK
Sage   GP02-SA: 3/4yd (70cm)
Batting:
100in x 100in (254cm x 254cm)
Quilting threads:
Dark red hand quilting thread

Templates:
see page 102

GGG

PATCH SHAPES
A single diamond patch shape (Template GGG) is used for this quilt. The diamonds are pieced into 8 segments, which are joined to make the quilt. The fabrics are used in sequence to produce dramatic rings of colour. The quilt is trimmed to a square shape rather than using many small templates for filling the edges.

CUTTING OUT
The Organic Stripe and Swiggle fabrics have four distinct design elements across the width of the fabric. These have been separated by cutting the patch shapes down the length of the fabric. 1 Design Element or 2 Design Elements alternated (on the outer rings) are used per ring of diamonds. Refer to the photograph to identify the individual design elements and their position.

Template GGG: Fabrics GP02-J, GP02-PG, GP02-SA and GP20-SL. Cut 2 3/4in (7cm) wide strips across the width of the fabric. Each strip will give you 10 patches per 45in (114cm) wide fabric. Cut 112 in GP02-SA, 104 in GP20-SL, 80 in GP02-PG and 64 in GP02-J.

Template GGG: Fabrics GP21-BL, GP21-BR, GP21-GN, GP22-GN and GP22-OC. Cut 2 3/4in (7cm) wide strips down the length of the fabric, separating the design elements as you cut.

Cut a total of 352 in GP22-OC (120 in Design Element 3, 96 in Design Element 1, 72 in Design Element 2, 64 in Design Element 4).

Cut a total of 240 in GP21-GN (88 in Design Element 3, 80 in Design Element 1, 56 in Design Element 2, 16 in Design Element 4).

Cut a total of 200 in GP21-BL (76 in Design Element 1, 32 in Design Element 2, 52 in Design Element 3, 40 in Design Element 4). Design Elements 1 and 3 are alternated in ring 13 counting from the centre out.

Cut a total of 168 in GP21-BR (120 in Design Element 3, 48 in Design Element 2).

Cut a total of 72 in GP22-GN (40 in Design Element 2, 24 in Design Element 3, 8 in Design Element 1).

Binding: Cut 10 strips 2 1/2in (6.25cm) wide x width of fabric in GP02-SA.
Backing: Cut 2 pieces 100in x 45in (254cm x 114cm) and 1 piece 100in x 13in (254cm x 33cm) in GP02-PG.

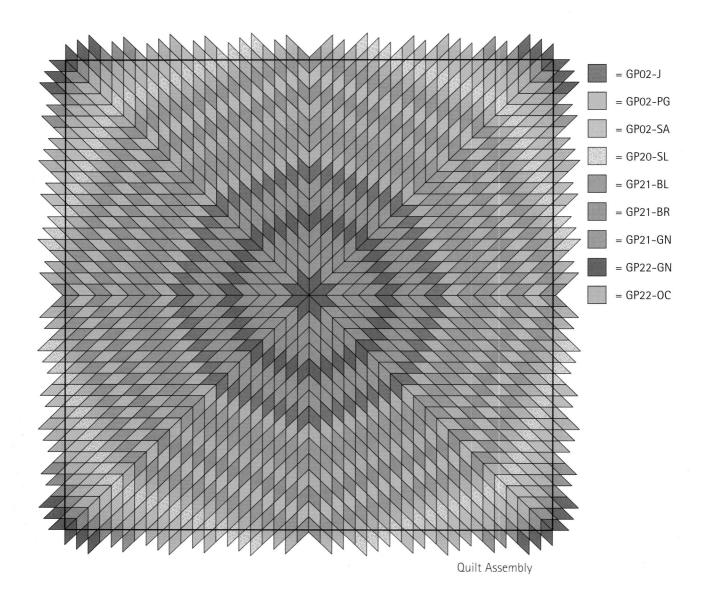

= GP02-J

= GP02-PG

= GP02-SA

= GP20-SL

= GP21-BL

= GP21-BR

= GP21-GN

= GP22-GN

= GP22-OC

Quilt Assembly

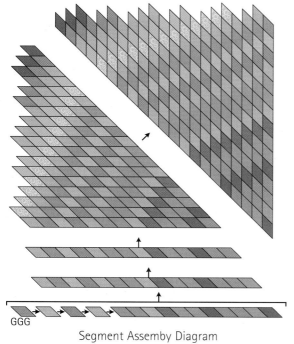

GGG

Segment Assemby Diagram

Timmed Quilt Diagram

MAKING THE QUILT

Using a 1/4in (6mm) seam allowance throughout and referring to the quilt assembly diagram and photograph for fabric placement, piece the diamonds into rows as shown in the segment assembly diagram (the rows are generous as the edges will be trimmed later). Join the rows to form 2 segments. Join the 2 segments as shown to form a quarter of the quilt. Make 4 quarters and join to make the quilt as shown in the quilt assembly diagram.

Mark a line onto the quilt with a washable marker or masking tape as shown in the quilt assembly diagram. At this stage trim the quilt edge about 1 inch (2.5cm) outside the marked line, this makes handling the quilt easier for layering and basting, don't worry if there a few gaps in the edge as final trimming will take place after the quilting is completed. The trimmed quilt diagram shows how the quilt will look after quilting and final trimming.

FINISHING THE QUILT

Press the quilt top. Seam the backing pieces using a 1/4in (6mm) seam allowance to form a piece approx. 100in x 100in (254cm x 254cm). Layer the quilt top, batting and backing and baste together (see page 112).
Hand quilt with dark red hand quilting thread as shown in the quilting diagram which shows a quarter of the quilt. Trim the quilt edges leaving a 1/4in (6mm) seam allowance outside the marked line and attach the binding (see page 113).

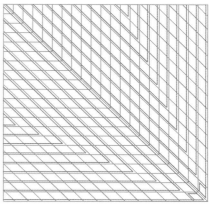

Quilting Diagram

Hot Sauce Quilt ★★

LIZA PRIOR LUCY

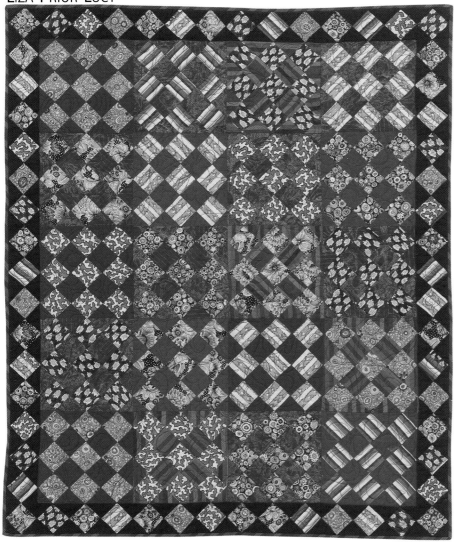

Liza has 'fussy cut' the ochre swiggle fabric to make the most of the four distinct design elements. A clever choice of prune shot cotton gives definition to the border.

SIZE OF QUILT
The finished quilt will measure approx. 40in x 48in (102cm x 122cm).

MATERIALS
Patchwork Fabrics:
ROMAN GLASS
Gold   GP01-G: ¼yd (25cm)
DAMASK
Plum Gold   GP02-PG: ¼yd (25cm)
FRUIT BASKET
Red   GP19-RD: ⅝yd (60cm)
PAPERWEIGHT
Pumpkin   GP20-PN: ¼yd (25cm)
SWIGGLE
Ochre   GP22-OC: ¾yd (70cm)

NARROW STRIPE
              NS 01: ⅜yd (35cm)
SHOT COTTON
Prune   SC 03: ½yd (45cm)
Persimmon   SC 07: ⅜yd (35cm)
Bittersweet   SC 10: ⅜yd (35cm)
Backing Fabric:
DAMASK
Plum Gold   GP02-PG: 1½yd (1.4m)
Bias Binding:
NARROW STRIPE
              NS 01: ½yd (45cm)

Batting:
44in x 52in (112cm x 132cm).
Quilting threads:
Maroon machine quilting thread.

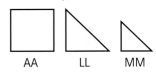

Templates:
see page 107

AA   LL   MM

PATCH SHAPES
One simple square patch shape (Template AA) is pieced 'on point' into blocks, the edges of which are filled using a triangle patch shape (Template LL) and the corners are completed with a second triangle patch shape (Template MM). The borders for this quilt are constructed using the same shapes (Templates AA, LL and MM).

CUTTING OUT
The Ochre Swiggle fabric (GP22-OC) has four distinct design elements. These have been separated and individually numbered in the quilt assembly diagram. However, which design element you assign to each number is not important. Liza split the fabrics for the blocks into two groups; GP01-G, GP02-PG, GP20-PN and GP22-OC are the 'foreground fabrics'; GP19-RD, NS 01, SC 07 and SC 10 are the 'background fabrics'. Whilst we have drawn the diagram as Liza's quilt was pieced, she emphasized that the combination of fore and background fabrics are very much your individual choice.
Template AA: Cut 2½in (6.5cm) wide strips across the width of the fabric. Each strip will give you 17 patches per 45in (114cm) wide fabric.
Cut 36 in GP22-OC Design Element 1, 34 in GP22-OC Design Element 2, GP22-OC Design Element 4, 25 in GP22-OC Design Element 3, 38 in GP20-PN. 36 in GP02-PG, 35 in GP01-G, 32 in GP19-RD, 16 in NS 01, SC 07 and SC 10.
Template LL: Cut 4in (10.25cm) wide strips across the width of the fabric. Each strip will give you 40 patches per 45in (114cm) wide fabric. Cut the strips into 4in (10.25cm) squares and cut each square diagonally twice. This ensures there are no bias edges along the sides of the quilt and blocks.
Cut 112 in SC 03, 64 in GP19-RD, 32 in NS 01, SC 07 and SC 10.
Template MM: Cut 2⅜in (6cm) wide strips across the width of the fabric. Each strip will give you 16 patches per 45in (114cm).

Quilt Assembly

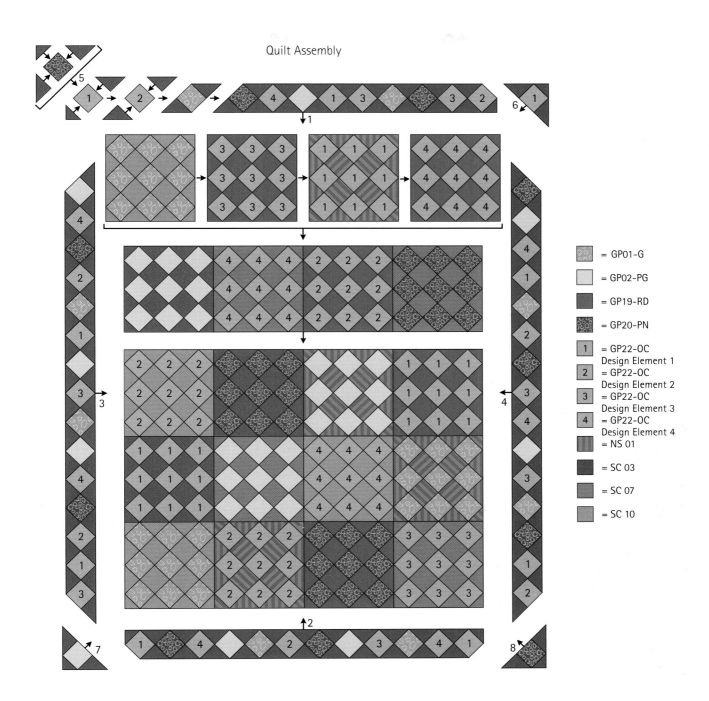

Legend:
- = GP01-G
- = GP02-PG
- = GP19-RD
- = GP20-PN
- 1 = GP22-OC Design Element 1
- 2 = GP22-OC Design Element 2
- 3 = GP22-OC Design Element 3
- 4 = GP22-OC Design Element 4
- = NS 01
- = SC 03
- = SC 07
- = SC 10

Cut 32 in GP19-RD, 16 in NS 01, SC 07, SC 10 and 8 in SC 03.

Binding: Cut 5¼yds (4.8m) of 2½in (6.5cm) wide bias binding in NS 01.

Backing: Cut 1 piece 44in x 52in (112cm x 132cm) in GP02-PG.

MAKING THE QUILT

Using a ¼in (6mm) seam allowance throughout, piece a total of 20 blocks as shown in the block assembly diagram. Piece the blocks into 5 rows of 4 blocks. Join the rows to form the quilt centre.

ADDING THE BORDERS

Piece the border sections as shown in the quilt assembly diagram and add to the quilt centre in the order indicated. The corner sections are added last.

FINISHING THE QUILT

Press the quilt top. Layer the quilt top, batting and backing and baste together (see page 112). Using a maroon machine quilting thread, quilt in a loose meandering pattern across the surface of the quilt. Trim the quilt edges and attach the binding (see page113).

Block Assembly

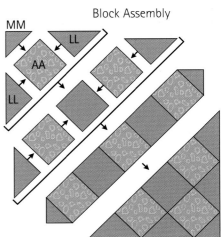

Rippled Diamonds Quilt ★ ★ ★

BRANDON MABLY

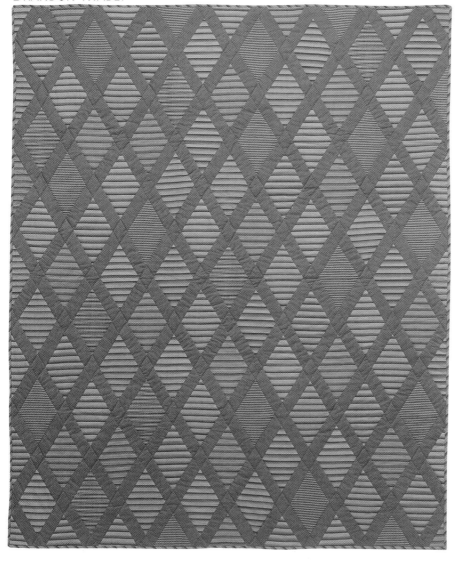

Brandon has taken a simple arrangement of large diamonds in pale, subtle, striped fabrics. The effect is like ripples on water.

SIZE OF QUILT
The finished quilt will measure approx.
67in x 87in (170cm x 221cm).

MATERIALS
Patchwork Fabrics:
BLUE AND WHITE STRIPE

BWS 01: ⁵/₈yd (60cm)
BWS 02: ³/₈yd (35cm)

OMBRE STRIPE

OS 01: ³/₄yd (70cm)
OS 02: ³/₄yd (70cm)
OS 04: ³/₄yd (70cm)
OS 05: ³/₄yd (70cm)

SHOT COTTON
Lilac SC 36: 3yds (2.75m)
Backing Fabric:
NARROW STRIPE

NS 16: 5¹/₈yds (4.7m)

Bias Binding:
OMBRE STRIPE

OS 04: ⁵/₈yd (60cm)

Batting:
71in x 91in (180cm x 231cm).
Quilting thread:
Toning machine quilting thread.

Templates:
see page 108

PATCH SHAPES
Based around a large diamond patch shape (Template CC) this quilt is sashed in a single shot cotton for a striking effect. The edges of the quilt are filled in using three triangle patch shapes (Templates DD, EE and FF). Two main sashing strips are used (Templates GG and HH) with three further sashing strips (Templates II, JJ and KK) used to fill in along the quilt edges. The templates for this quilt as printed at 50% of true size. Photocopy at 200% before using.
Note: All the fabrics that Brandon chose for this project are reversible, however if you choose non reversible fabrics you will need to make additional 'reverse' templates for Shapes EE and II.

CUTTING OUT
Note: Refer to the quilt assembly diagram for stripe direction.
Template CC: Cut 17 in OS 04, 16 in OS 02, OS 05, 15 in OS 01, 12 in BWS01 and 7 in BWS02.
Template DD: Cut 4 in BWS01, OS 05, 3 in OS 01, 2 in OS 04 and 1 in OS 02.
Template EE: Cut 2 in OS 01, 1 in OS 02 and OS 05.
Template FF: Cut 3 in OS 02, OS 05, 2 in OS 04, 1 in BWS01 and OS 01.
Template GG: Cut 2¹/₂in (6.5cm) wide strips across the width of the fabric. Each strip will give you 6 patches per 45in (114cm) wide fabric. Cut 84 in SC 36.
Template HH: Cut 2¹/₂in (6.5cm) wide strips across the width of the fabric. Each strip will give you 4 patches per 45in (114cm) wide fabric. Cut 82 in SC 36.
Template II: Cut 2¹/₂in (6.5cm) wide strips across the width of the fabric. Each strip will give you 4 patches per 45in (114cm) wide fabric. Cut 10 in SC 36.
Template JJ: Cut 2¹/₂in (6.5cm) wide strips across the width of the fabric. Each strip will give you 4 patches per 45in (114cm) wide fabric. Cut 2 in SC 36.

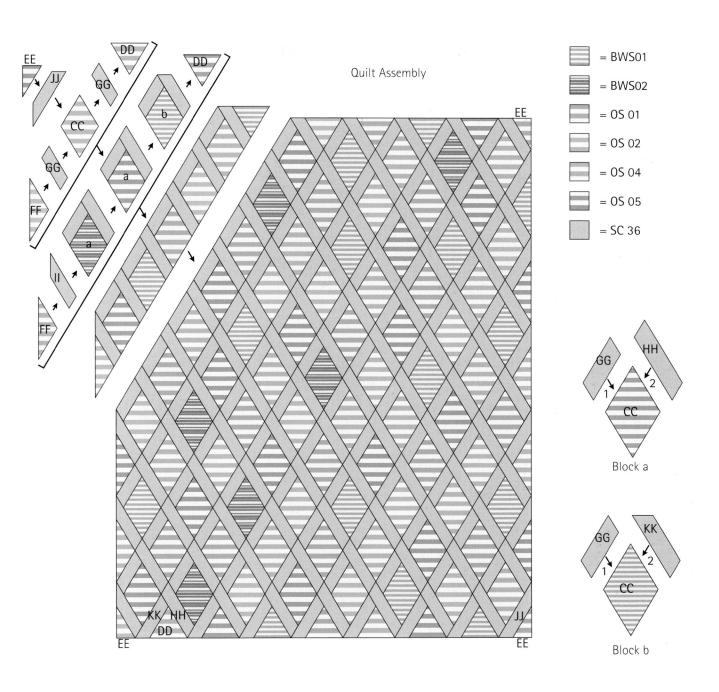

Quilt Assembly

Legend:
- = BWS01
- = BWS02
- = OS 01
- = OS 02
- = OS 04
- = OS 05
- = SC 36

Block a

Block b

Template KK: Cut 2¹/₂in (6.5cm) wide strips across the width of the fabric. Each strip will give you 5 patches per 45in (114cm) wide fabric. Cut 14 in SC 36.

Binding: Cut 9yds (8.2m) of 2¹/₂in (6.5cm) wide bias binding from OS 04.

Backing: Cut 1 piece 91in x 44in (231cm x 112cm) and 1 piece 91in x 28in (231cm x 71cm) in NS 16.

MAKING THE QUILT
Using a ¹/₄in (6mm) seam allowance throughout, piece 75 of block a and 7 of block b as shown in the block assembly diagram referring to the quilt assembly diagram for fabric placement. Lay out the pieced blocks as shown in the quilt assembly diagram completing the quilt edges as shown. Separate the diagonal rows and carefully stitch together. Join the rows to complete the quilt top.

FINISHING THE QUILT
Press the quilt top. Seam the backing pieces using a ¹/₄in (6mm) seam allowance to form a piece approx 71in x 91in (180cm x 231cm). Layer the quilt top, batting and backing and baste together (see page 112). Using a toning machine quilting thread, quilt in the ditch along the diagonal seam lines. Trim the quilt edges and attach the binding (see page 113).

Beaded Curtain Quilt ★★

KAFFE FASSETT

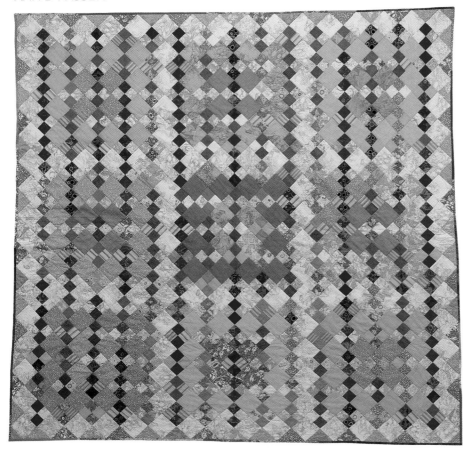

I saw this vintage American quilt at the Houston Quilt Festival. It made me think of strings of beads in an old fashioned door curtain.

SIZE OF QUILT
The finished quilt will measure approx.
90½in x 90½in (230cm x 230cm).

MATERIALS
Patchwork Fabrics:
Note: The vertical rows which depict the 'beads' in Kaffe's design are detailed exactly in the diagram. The horizontal rows are left blank as they were filled with a soft colourwash of shades, examples of the fabrics used are detailed below, but you could include leftover fabrics from other Rowan projects.

ROMAN GLASS
Jewel	GP01-J:	1/8yd (15cm)
Red	GP01-R:	1/8yd (15cm)
Stones	GP01-S:	1/8yd (15cm)

DAMASK
Jewel	GP02-J:	1/4yd (25cm)

CHRYSANTHEMUM
Ochre	GP13-O:	1/4yd (25cm)

DOTTY
Lavender	GP14-L:	3/8yd (35cm)
Ochre	GP14-O:	1/2yd (45cm)
Sea Green	GP14-SG:	1/8yd (15cm)
Terracotta	GP14-T:	1/2yd (45cm)

BUBBLES
Plum	GP15-P:	1/4yd (25cm)

PEONY
Blue	GP17-BL:	1/4yd (25cm)
Green	GP17-GN:	1/4yd (25cm)
Maroon	GP17-MR:	1/8yd (15cm)
Ochre	GP17-OC:	3/8yd (35cm)
Red	GP17-RD:	1/4yd (25cm)
Violet	GP17-VI:	1/4yd (25cm) or use leftover from backing

FRUIT BASKET
Apricot	GP19-AP:	3/8yd (35cm)
Pink	GP19-PK:	1 3/4yd (1.6m)
Red	GP19-RD:	1/4yd (25cm)
Taupe	GP19-TA:	1/4yd (25cm)
Teal	GP19-TE:	1/8yd (15cm)

SHOT COTTON
Ginger	SC 01:	1/8yd (15cm)
Bittersweet	SC 10:	1/8yd (15cm)
Lavender	SC 14:	1/4yd (25cm)
Mustard	SC 16:	1/8yd (15cm)
Lichen	SC 19:	1/4yd (25cm)
Ecru	SC 24:	1/2yd (45cm)
Duck Egg	SC 26:	3/8yd (35cm)
Mushroom	SC 31:	1/4yd (25cm)
Rosy	SC 32:	1/2yd (45cm)
Watermelon	SC 33:	1/4yd (25cm)
Lilac	SC 36:	1/4yd (25cm)
Coffee	SC 37:	1/8yd (15cm)
Biscuit	SC 38:	3/8yd (35cm)

OTHER 'LIGHT' FABRICS
A total of 2 yds (1.8m) in pale pink, lilac, lavender, blue, green. Examples of fabrics used:
Roman Glass Pink	GP01-PK
Roman Glass Pastel	GP01-PT
Forget-me-not Rose Circus	GP08-C
Damask Pastel	GP02-P
Peony Violet	GP17-VI
(use leftover from backing)	
Peony Grey	GP17-GR
Fruit Basket Blue	GP19-BL
Blue and White Stripe 2	BWS02
Ombre Stripe 2	OS02

Backing Fabric:
PEONY
Violet	GP17-VI: 8yds (7.3m)

Binding Fabric:
Pieced from leftover fabric.
Batting:
95in x 95in (241cm x 241cm)
Quilting thread:
Toning machine quilting thread.

Templates:
see page 105

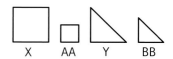

X   AA   Y   BB

PATCH SHAPES
A small square patch shape (Template AA) is used to piece four patch blocks which are then alternated with large square patch shapes (Template X), in diagonal rows. The edges of the quilt are filled using a large triangle patch shape (Template Y) and the extreme corners of the quilt are completed with a small triangle patch shape (Template BB).

CUTTING OUT
Template X: Cut 4½in (11.5cm) wide strips across the width of the fabric. Each strip will give you 9 patches per 45in (114cm) wide fabric. Cut 112 in GP19-PK, 24 in SC 24, SC 32, 23 in GP14-O, 16 in GP14-T, 15 in GP19-AP, 12 in SC 38, 9 in GP17-OC, 4 in GP17-RD, GP17-VI, GP19-TA, SC 26, SC 36 and 1 in GP13-O.

Template AA: Cut 2½in (6.5cm) wide strips across the width of the fabric. Each strip will give you 17 patches per 45in (114cm) wide fabric. Cut 450 from the 'light' fabric selection, 47 in SC 19, 38 in GP19-RD, 34 in GP17-GN, 30 in GP02-J, 29 in SC 14, 28 in SC 26, 27 in GP15-P, 26 in GP14-L, SC 33, 23 in GP17-BL, 20 in SC 31, 17 in GP17-MR, 16 in GP19-TE,

14 in SC 01, 13 in SC 10, 12 in GP01-J, GP01-R, 10 in GP17-RD, 9 in SC 37, 7 in GP01-S, SC 16, 4 in GP14-SG and 1 in GP17-VI.

Template Y: Cut 3⅜in (8.5cm) wide strips across the width of the fabric. Cutting the fabric this way avoids bias cuts along the quilt edges. Each strip will give you 11 patches per 45in (114cm) wide fabric.

Quilt Assembly

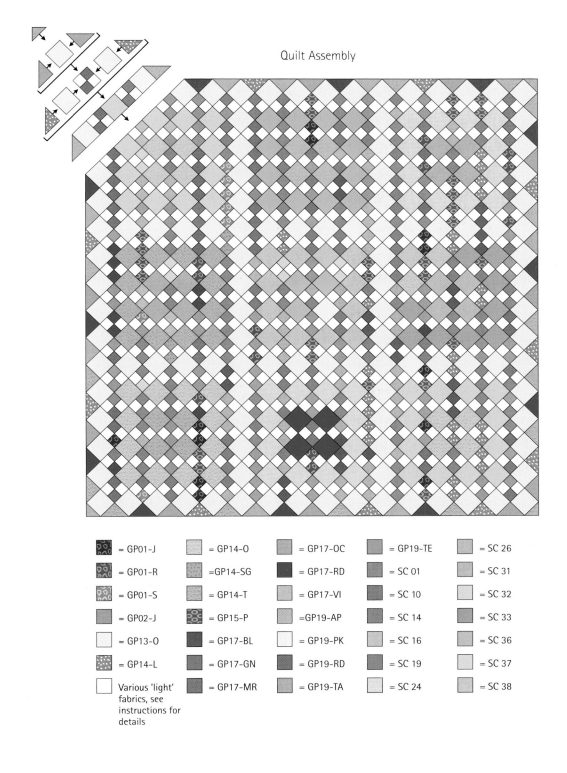

= GP01-J	= GP14-O	= GP17-OC	= GP19-TE	= SC 26
= GP01-R	=GP14-SG	= GP17-RD	= SC 01	= SC 31
= GP01-S	= GP14-T	= GP17-VI	= SC 10	= SC 32
= GP02-J	= GP15-P	=GP19-AP	= SC 14	= SC 33
= GP13-O	= GP17-BL	= GP19-PK	= SC 16	= SC 36
= GP14-L	= GP17-GN	= GP19-RD	= SC 19	= SC 37
Various 'light' fabrics, see instructions for details	= GP17-MR	= GP19-TA	= SC 24	= SC 38

Cut 16 in GP14-T, 12 in GP14-L, GP17-OC, GP17-RD and 8 in GP19-TA.
Template BB: Cut 3³/₄in (9.5cm) wide strips across the width of the fabric. Each strip will give you 22 patches per 45in (114cm) wide fabric. Cut 2 in GP14-T and GP19-TA.

Binding: Cut strips 2¹/₂in (6.25cm) wide strips from leftover fabric. Piece into a long strip 10¹/₂yds (9.6m).

Backing: Cut 2 pieces 95in x 44in (242cm by 112cm) and 1 piece 95in x 8in (242cm by 20cm) in GP17-VI.

MAKING THE QUILT
Using a ¹/₄in (6mm) seam allowance throughout, piece a total of 450 four-patch blocks as shown in block assembly diagrams a, b and c. Refer to the quilt assembly diagram for colour selection, filling in the 'blank' squares from the 'light' fabric selections as specified above. Join the blocks into diagonal rows alternating with the template X squares, again referring to the quilt assembly diagram for fabric placement. Complete the ends of the rows with the template Y triangles and the extreme corners of the quilt with the template BB triangles.

FINISHING THE QUILT
Press the quilt top. Seam the backing pieces using a ¹/₄in (6mm) seam allowance to form a piece approx. 95in x 95in (241cm x 241cm). Layer the quilt top, batting and backing and baste together (see page 112). Using a toning machine quilting thread, quilt in the ditch along the diagonal seam lines. Trim the quilt edges and attach the binding (see page 113).

Block Assembly

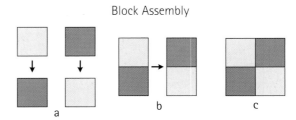

a   b   c

Canyon Star Quilt ★★★

Kaffe Fassett

I noticed this layout for a star called Flat Iron. As I gathered the pink and duck egg elements of the palette together it reminded me of the USA's South West where canyons are common, hence the name.

SIZE OF QUILT
The finished quilt will measure approx.
69¹/₂in x 91in (176.5cm x 231cm).

MATERIALS
Patchwork Fabrics:
ROMAN GLASS
Gold	GP01-G:	³/₄yd (70cm)
Pastel	GP01-P:	³/₈yd (35cm)
Pink	GP01-PK:	⁵/₈yd (60cm)

DAMASK
Plum Gold	GP02-PG:	³/₈yd (35cm)

ARTICHOKES
Jewel	GP07-J:	³/₈yd (35cm)
Leafy	GP07-L:	¹/₄yd (25cm)

FORGET-ME-NOT ROSE
Jewel	GP08-J:	¹/₂yd (45cm)

CHRYSANTHEMUM
Red	GP13-R:	⁵/₈yd (60cm)

DOTTY
Ochre	GP14-O:	¹/₂yd (45cm)
Sea Green	GP14-SG:	³/₈yd (35cm)

PEONY
Maroon	GP17-MR:	³/₄yd (70cm)

FRUIT BASKET
Apricot	GP19-AP:	³/₈yd (35cm)
Red	GP19-RD:	⁵/₈yd (60cm) or use leftover from backing.

ALTERNATE STRIPE
	AS 10:	³/₈yd (35cm)

BROAD STRIPE
	BS 11:	1 yd (90cm) includes binding

DOUBLE IKAT CHECKERBOARD
Gold	DiC 04:	¹/₄yd (25cm)

DOUBLE IKAT POLKA
Pumpkin	DiP 02:	⁵/₈yd (60cm)

SINGLE IKAT WASH
Red	SiW 06:	¹/₂yd (45cm)

SHOT COTTON
Duck Egg	SC 26:	³/₈yd (35cm)
Rosy	SC 32:	1 yd (90cm)
Apple	SC 39:	¹/₂yd (45cm)

Backing Fabric:
FRUIT BASKET
Red	GP19-RD:	5¹/₂yds (5m)

Binding Fabric:
BROAD STRIPE
	BS 11:	see patchwork fabrics

Batting:
74in x 95in (188cm x 242cm).

Quilting thread:
Perle cotton thread in soft pink.

Templates:
see pages 101, 106

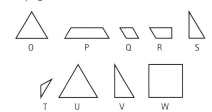

PATCH SHAPES
The centre of this quilt is pieced from blocks constructed around an equilateral triangle patch shape (Template O), which is extended using a lozenge patch shape (Template P) and a diamond patch shape (Template Q). These blocks are joined in diagonal rows. Along the top and bottom of the quilt edge a second 'half' block is used to fill in. This is constructed from templates P and Q as above plus 2 triangle shapes (template S) which is reversed as necessary (template T) and a lozenge shape (template R) which is also reversed

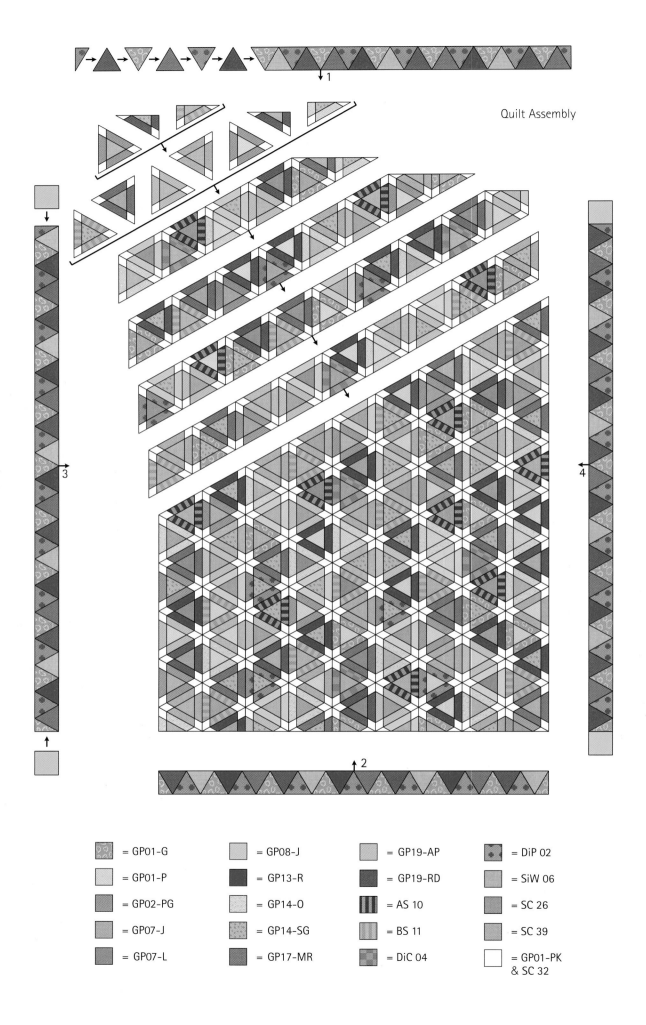

Quilt Assembly

= GP01-G = GP08-J = GP19-AP = DiP 02

= GP01-P = GP13-R = GP19-RD = SiW 06

= GP02-PG = GP14-O = AS 10 = SC 26

= GP07-J = GP14-SG = BS 11 = SC 39

= GP07-L = GP17-MR = DiC 04 = GP01-PK
& SC 32

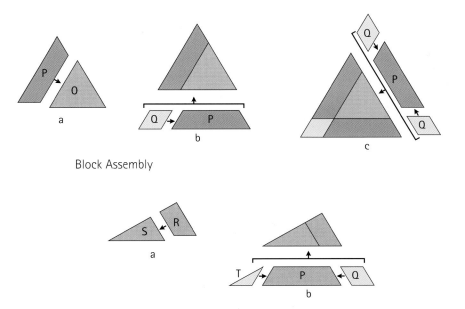

Block Assembly

Half Block Assembly

as necessary. This quilt also has a pieced border, again using an equilateral triangle patch shape (Template U), with a further triangle patch shape for the ends of the rows (Template V). The extreme corners of the quilt are completed with a simple square patch shape (Template W).

CUTTING OUT

Template O: Cut 3⁷/₈in (9.75cm) wide strips across the width of the fabric. Each strip will give you 18 patches per 45in (114cm) wide fabric. Cut 49 in SC39, 37 in GP14-SG, GP01-P, 36 in SC 26 and 21 in GP07-L.

Template P: Cut 1³/₄in (4.5cm) wide strips across the width of the fabric. Each strip will give you 8 patches per 45in (114cm) wide fabric. Cut 57 in GP14-O, 52 in GP19-AP, 50 in GP17-MR, 47 in GP08-J, 46 in BS 11, 44 in GP07-J, 43 in GP02-PG, GP13-R, 42 in GP01-G, 38 in GP19-RD, 36 in AS 10, 21 in DiP 02, SiW 06 and 18 in DiC 04.

Template Q: Cut 1³/₄in (4.5cm) wide strips across the width of the fabric. Each strip will give you 20 patches per 45in (114cm) wide fabric. Cut 370 in SC 32 and 188 in GP01-PK.

Template R: Cut 1³/₄in (4.5cm) wide strips across the width of the fabric. Each strip will give you 14 patches per 45in (114cm) wide fabric, reversing template

as necessary. Cut 3 in GP01-G, GP14-O, 2 in GP07-J, GP08-J, GP17-MR, GP19-RD, 1 in GP02-PG, GP13-R, GP19-AP and BS 11.

Template S: Cut 2¹/₂in (6.5cm) wide strips across the width of the fabric. Each strip will give you 18 patches per 45in (114cm) wide fabric, reversing template as necessary. Cut 10 in SC 39, 6 in GP13-R and 2 in SC 26.

Template T: Cut 1¹/₄in (3.25cm) wide strips across the width of the fabric. Each strip will give you 18 patches per 45in (114cm) wide fabric. Cut 10 in SC 32 and 8 in GP01-PK.

Template U: Cut 4⁵/₈in (11.75cm) wide strips across the width of the fabric. Each strip will give you 15 patches per 45in (114cm) wide fabric. Cut 31 in GP01-G, DiP02, 17 in GP17-MR, GP19-RD, 16 in GP13-R and SiW 06.

Template V: Cut 2⁷/₈in (7.5cm) wide strips across the width of the fabric. Each strip will give you 16 patches per 45in (114cm) wide fabric. Cut 4 in GP01-G and DiP 02.

Template W: Cut 4³/₈in (11.25cm) wide strips across the width of the fabric. Each strip will give you 9 patches per 45in (114cm) wide fabric. Cut 4 in GP08-J.

Binding: Cut 8 strips 2¹/₂in (6.25cm) wide x width of fabric in BS 11.

Backing: Cut 1 piece 95in x 44in (242cm by 112cm) and 1 piece 95in x 31in (242cm by 79cm) in GP19-RD.

MAKING THE QUILT

Using a ¹/₄in (6mm) seam allowance throughout, piece 180 blocks as shown in block assembly diagrams a, b and c, and 18 half blocks as shown in half block assembly diagrams a and b. Refer to the quilt assembly diagram for fabric placement. Join the blocks into diagonal rows as shown in the quilt assembly diagram filling in the quilt top and bottom edge with the half blocks.

ADDING THE BORDERS

Piece the borders referring to the quilt assembly diagram for fabric placement. Working with triangles can be a little tricky and your quilt may turn out a little larger or smaller than expected so, measure the quilt centre and trim or extend the borders as necessary. Add the borders in the order indicated in the quilt assembly diagram.

FINISHING THE QUILT

Press the quilt top. Seam the backing pieces using a ¹/₄in (6mm) seam allowance to form a piece approx. 74in x 95in (188cm x 242cm). Layer the quilt top, batting and backing and baste together (see page 112). Using a soft pink perle cotton thread, hand quilt in the ditch to outline each of the pink stars as shown in the quilting diagram. Trim the quilt edges and attach the binding (see page 113).

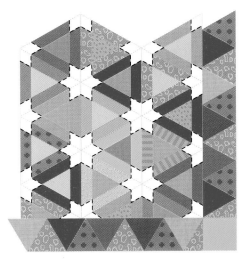

Quilting Diagram

Whimsical Basket Quilt ★★★

BETSY MENNESSON

I used three different printed stripe fabrics from Kaffe Fassett's prints. This gave me lots to choose from in one fabric, I used the different design elements as though they were different fabrics.

SIZE OF QUILT
The finished quilt will measure approx. 70in x 70in (178cm x 178cm).

MATERIALS
Patchwork Fabrics:
ROMAN GLASS
Pink	GP01-PK:	1/4yd (25cm)
Leafy	GP01-L:	3/8yd (35cm)
Red	GP01-R:	1/4yd (25cm)

FLORAL DANCE
Magenta	GP12-MG:	1/4yd (25cm)

AUGUST ROSES
Magenta	GP18-MG:	1 1/8yd (1m)
Pink	GP18-PK:	1/2yd (45cm)

ORGANIC STRIPE
Lime	GP21-LM:	1/2yd (45cm)
Pink	GP21-PK:	1/2yd (45cm)

SWIGGLE
Pink	GP22-PK:	1 1/2yd (1.4m)

SHOT COTTON
Sunshine	SC 35:	1/8yd (15cm)
Apple	SC 39:	2 yds (1.8m)

Backing Fabric:
SHOT COTTON
Raspberry	SC 08:	see below
Chartreuse	SC 12:	see below
Watermelon	SC 33:	see below
Apple	SC 39:	see below
	Total	4 1/4yds (3.9m)

Binding Fabric:
AUGUST ROSES
Magenta		GP18-MG: see patchwork fabrics

Batting:
74in x 74in (188cm x 188cm).

Quilting thread:
Toning machine quilting thread.

Templates:
see pages 99, 100, 102, 105, 107

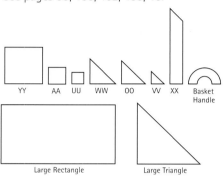

PATCH SHAPES
The quilt is formed by a large central block surrounded by 7 borders. The central section is a pieced basket using 2 triangle patch shapes (Templates VV and WW) and 1 lozenge patch shape (Template XX); these are pieced into the body of the basket, which is then made into a large square by the addition of 2 large triangles cut to size and a large rectangle cut to size. The first simple border is then added. The second border is pieced using 1 square patch shape (Template UU) these are pieced into four patch blocks and 1 triangle patch shape (Template OO). These borders are extended to fit with simple cut strips. The third border is simple strips. The fourth border is simple strips with naive appliqué and square corner posts (Template YY). The fifth border is pieced from strips of fabric, cut to random lengths with mitred corners. The sixth border is pieced from 1 square patch shape (Template AA). The final border is simple strips with mitred corners.

CUTTING OUT
Notes: Betsy chose to 'fussy cut' the Swiggle fabric which has 4 different design elements across the width. The diagrams are numbered 1-4 to represent the 4 elements, refer to the diagrams and photograph for placement.
The fabric that Betsy chose for block background is reversible, however if you choose non reversible fabrics you will need to make an additional 'reverse' template for Shape XX.

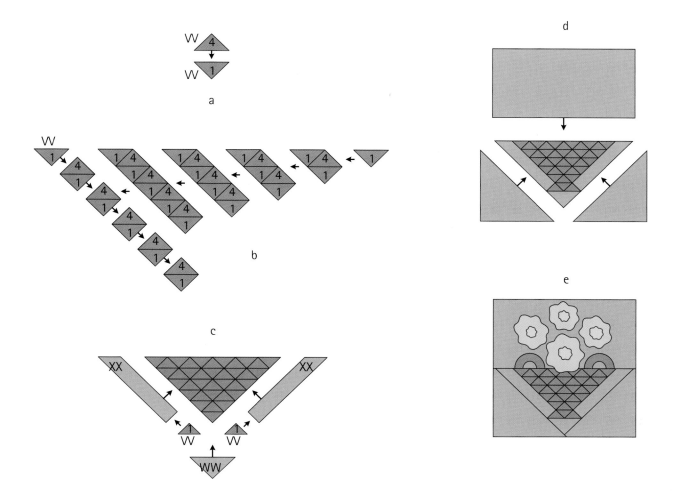

The sixth border can be pieced from cut squares, or the piecing can be speeded up by stitching 4 strips of fabric into strip sets and cutting 2¹/₂in (6.5cm) slices; these are then pieced into the borders.

Template AA: Cut 2¹/₂in (6.5cm) wide strips across the width of the fabric. Each strip will give you 17 patches per 45in (114cm) wide fabric. Cut 232 in SC 39, 78 in GP21-LM, 76 in GP21-PK, 50 in GP18-PK and 28 in GP01-PK. Alternatively stitch the strips into strip sets and cut 2¹/₂in (6.5cm) wide slices.
Template OO: Cut 2³/₄in (7cm) wide strips across the width of the fabric. Each strip will give you 14 patches per 45in (114cm) wide fabric. Cut 24 in GP22-PK Design Element 4.
Template UU: Cut 2in (5cm) wide strips across the width of the fabric. Each strip will give you 21 patches per 45in (114cm) wide fabric. Cut 24 in GP21-LM and SC 35.
Template VV: Cut 2¹/₂in (6.5cm) wide strips across the width of the fabric. Each strip will give you 34 patches per

45in (114cm) wide fabric. Cut 23 in GP22-PK Design Element 1 and 15 in GP22-PK Design Element 4.
Template WW: Cut 3in (7.5cm) wide strips Cut 1 in SC 39.
Template XX: Cut 2¹/₈in (5.5cm) wide strips. Cut 2 in SC 39.
Template YY: Cut 5¹/₄in (13.25cm) wide strips. Cut 4 in GP18-PK.
Large Rectangle: Cut 1 rectangle 20in x 10¹/₂in (51cm x 26.5cm)in SC 39.
Large Triangle: Cut 1 square 11in x 11in (28cm x 28cm) in SC 39.
Cut the square diagonally to form 2 triangles.
Appliqué Shapes: Cut 2 basket handles using the template provided.
If you are using the hand appliqué method add a ¹/₄in (6mm) seam allowance. If using a bonding agent follow the directions that come with the product you choose.
The flowers are freeform cut and we have not provided templates.
Cut 4 flowers and 4 flower centres. Also cut 16 x 1³/₄in (4.5cm) circles for border 4 appliqué in GP18-PK, adding seam allowance if using the hand appliqué

method and a total of 150in (380cm) x 1¹/₂in (3.75cm) wide bias cut vine.
Border 1: Cut 2 strips 19¹/₂in x 1¹/₂in (49.5cm x 3.75cm) and 2 strips 21¹/₂in x 1¹/₂in (54.5cm x 3.75cm) in GP22-PK Design Element 3.
Border 2: Cut 2 strips 9¹/₂in x 4¹/₂in (24.25cm x 11.5cm) and 2 strips 18in x 4¹/₂in (45.75cm x 11.5cm) in GP22-PK Design Element 4.
Border 3: Cut 2 strips 30in x 1¹/₂in (76.25cm x 3.75cm) and 2 strips 32in x 1¹/₂in (81.25cm x 3.75cm) in GP22-PK Design Element 3.
Border 4: Cut 4 strips 32in x 5¹/₄in (81.25cm x 13.5cm) in SC 39.
Border 5: Cut 2in (5cm) wide strips across the width of the fabric. You will need a total of 16 strips in GP01-R, GP12-MG, GP22-PK Design Element 1, GP22-PK Design Element 2 and GP22-PK Design Element 3.
Border 7: Cut 7 strips 2¹/₂in (6.5cm) wide strips across the width of the fabric in GP18-MG.

Binding: Cut 7 strips 2¹/₂in (6.5cm) wide strips across the width of the fabric in GP18-MG.

Backing: Betsy chose to piece the backing for this quilt.
She used very large rectangles and strips in SC 08, SC 12, SC 33 and SC 39.

MAKING THE QUILT

Using a ¼in (6mm) seam allowance throughout piece the basket section of the centre panel, as shown in block assembly diagrams a, b and c.
Next add the large rectangle and large triangles to form a large square as shown in block assembly diagram d.
Add the appliqué shapes, by hand or machine as shown in block assembly diagram e, making sure there is enough room around the shapes to trim the centre panel to 19½in (49.5cm) square, which should be done when the appliqué is complete.

Add border 1 as shown in quilt assembly diagram 1.
For border 2 make a total of 12 four patch blocks using the same method as shown for Beaded Curtain Quilt block

assembly diagrams a, b and c.
Piece these into strips by adding template OO triangles.
The position in the pieced sections is up to you, for the side borders take the take the 9½in x 4½in (24.25cm x 11.5cm) strips. Lay on the pieced section and cut the strip at a 45 degree angle so that the pieced section will fit between the cut edges. Stitch together to complete the border and add to the centre section. Repeat using the 18in x 4½in (45.75cm x 11.5cm) strips for the top and bottom borders. Add border 3 as shown in quilt assembly diagram 1.

Add border 4 as shown in quilt assembly diagram 2. Add the vines and circles using either hand or machine appliqué. An easy way to appliqué the vines is shown in the appliqué section in Patchwork Knowhow on page 111.

Border 5 is pieced using 2in (5cm) strips. Cut the strips into random lengths using quilt assembly diagram 2 as a guide.

Piece into 4 borders 52in x 5in (132cm x 12.75cm) unfinished size.
Add to the quilt sides and mitre referring to the Mitreing Borders section on pages 111 and 112.

Border 6 is pieced into 2 sections 4 x 25 squares for the quilt sides and 2 sections 4 x 33 squares for the quilt top and bottom.

Border 7 is added to the quilt sides and the corners mitred.
Refer to the Mitreing Borders section on pages 111 and 112, to complete the quilt.

FINISHING THE QUILT

Press the quilt top. Seam the backing pieces using a ¼in (6mm) seam allowance to form a piece approx. 74in x 74in (188cm x 188cm).
Layer the quilt top, batting and backing and baste together (see page 112).
Using a toning machine quilting thread quilt as shown in the quilting diagram. Trim the quilt edges and attach the binding (see page 113).

Quilting Diagram

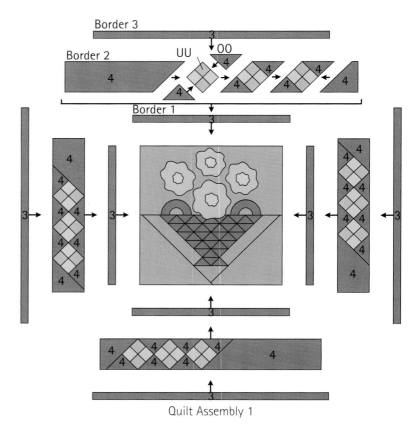

Quilt Assembly 1

Quilt Assembly 2

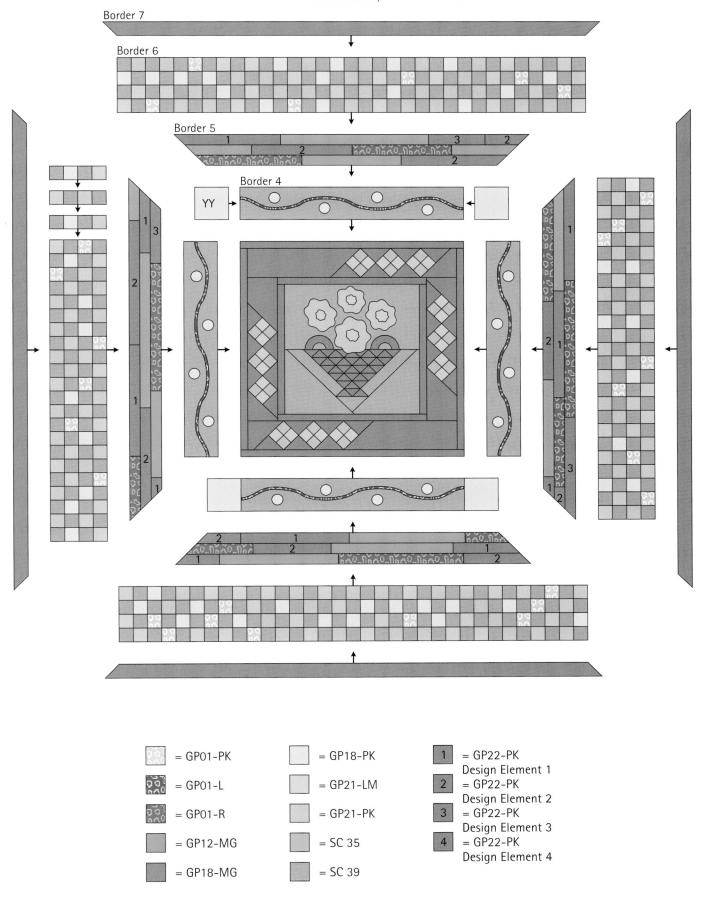

Border 7

Border 6

Border 5

Border 4

YY

= GP01-PK

= GP01-L

= GP01-R

= GP12-MG

= GP18-MG

= GP18-PK

= GP21-LM

= GP21-PK

= SC 35

= SC 39

1 = GP22-PK
Design Element 1

2 = GP22-PK
Design Element 2

3 = GP22-PK
Design Element 3

4 = GP22-PK
Design Element 4

Whimsical Basket - Betsy Mennesson

Zig Zag Bag - Pauline Smith

Zig Zag Bag ★

PAULINE SMITH

This richly coloured bag is quick and easy to make.

SIZE OF BAG
The finished bag will measure approx.
13³/₄in x 16¹/₂in (35cm x 42cm).

MATERIALS
Fabrics:
PEONY
Maroon   GP17-MR: ¹/₈yd (15cm)
PANSY
Brown   GP23-BR: ¹/₂yd (45cm)
                (includes straps and back)
DIAGONAL POPPY
Aubergine   GP24-AU: ¹/₈yd (15cm)
PACHRANGI STRIPE
                PS 13: ¹/₈yd (15cm)
SINGLE IKAT WASH
Banana   SiW 03: ¹/₈yd (15cm)
Red   SiW 06: ¹/₂yd (45cm)
                (includes lining)
SHOT COTTON
Opal   SC 05: ¹/₈yd (15cm)

Batting:
2 pieces 15in x 18in (38cm x 46cm), 2
pieces 22in x 2¹/₂in (56cm x 6.5cm)

Quilting thread:
Dark Maroon machine quilting thread.

Templates:
see page 102

PATCH SHAPES
The bag front is made from a single
triangle patch shape (template D), the
back is a single piece of print fabric. The
straps are padded for comfort.

CUTTING OUT
Template E: Cut 3⁵/₈in (9.25cm) wide
strips across the width of the fabric. Each
strip will give you 22 patches per 45in
(114cm) wide fabric.
Cut 13 in GP24-AU, 10 in SC 05, 9 in
GP17-MR, SiW 06, 8 in GP23-BR, 6 in
SiW 03 and 5 in PS 13.

Bag Back:
Cut 1 piece 14¹/₄in x 17in (36.25cm x
43.25cm) in GP23-BR.

Straps:
Cut 2 strips 22in x 2¹/₂in (56cm x 6.5cm)
in GP23-BR.

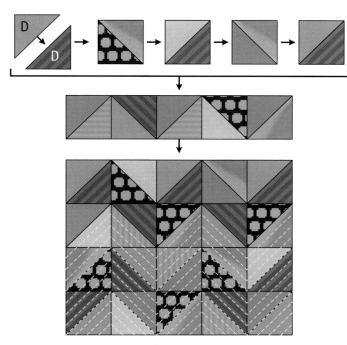

Bag Front Assembly

Bag Straps

= GP17-MR   = SiW 03

= GP23-BR   = SiW 06

= GP24-AU   = SC 05

= PS 13

Lining:
Cut 2 pieces 14¼in x 17in (36.25cm x 43.25cm) in SiW 06.

MAKING THE BAG FRONT
Using a ¼in (6mm) seam allowance throughout and referring to the bag front assembly diagram for colour placement, assemble the triangles into squares, then into 6 rows of 6 squares. Join the rows.

FINISHING THE BAG
1. Press the bag front and back, layer each with batting and baste together. Quilt the bag front as show in the bag front assembly diagram. The bag back was simply 'cross hatched' with diagonal quilting lines about 1¾in (4.5cm) apart, so that each quilted 'diamond' enclosed 4

pansies. Lay aside.
2. To make the straps, place 1 fabric strip right side up onto a batting strip, matching the edges carefully, baste and quilt 3 parallel lines along the length of the strip. The first up the centre of the strip and then the others ½in (1.25cm) offset to either side of the centre line. Next, fold the strap along the length with the fabric right sides together on the inside of the fold. Using a ¼in (6mm) seam allowance stitch along the length of the strap to make a tube with the batting on the outside, (don't trim the batting as it makes the finished strap soft and padded). Turn the tube through. Make 2.
3. Take the bag front and back, place right sides together and stitch together

along the sides and bottom, trim excess batting back to the seam line to reduce bulk. Leave the top edges free, turn the bag through. Baste one strap to the bag front and one to the back as shown in the bag strap diagram.
4. Take the lining pieces, seam along 2 long sides to form a tube. Place the bag inside the lining tube (right sides together) making sure the side seams and top edges are matched. Stitch around the top edge, using 2 rows of stitching across the straps for extra strength.
5. Turn the bag through and press a ¼in (6mm) hem to the raw edge of the lining. Stitch the lining bottom closed very close to the pressed edge. Tuck the lining inside the bag, press lightly and top stitch ¼in (6mm) from the top edge.

Ebay On Point Quilt ★

KAFFE FASSETT

I saw this idea as a vintage top on Ebay, the internet auction house. I love the very simple layout with lots of surprises to explore.

SIZE OF QUILT
The finished quilt will measure approx. 56½in x 73½in (143.5cm x 186.5cm).

MATERIALS
Patchwork Fabrics:
Note: The Organic Stripe and Swiggle fabrics have several different design elements across the width of the fabric. Kaffe chose to 'fussy cut' these fabrics, refer to the photograph for placement. Where necessary 2 fabric quantities are specified, the first does not allow for fussy cutting, the second does.

ROMAN GLASS
Red	GP01-R:	¼yd (25cm)

DAMASK
Pastel	GP02-P:	¼yd (25cm)
Sage	GP02-SA:	¼yd (25cm)

DOTTY
Lavender	GP14-L:	¼yd (25cm)
Sea Green	GP14-SG:	¼yd (25cm)
Terracotta	GP14-T:	¼yd (25cm)

MOSAIC
Grey	GP16-GR:	¼yd (25cm)
Pink	GP16-PK:	¼yd (25cm)

PEONY
Blue	GP17-BL:	¼yd (25cm)
Green	GP17-GN:	¼yd (25cm)
Grey	GP17-GR:	¼yd (25cm)
Red	GP17-RD:	¼yd (25cm)
Violet	GP17-VI:	¼yd (25cm)

FRUIT BASKET
Taupe	GP19-TA:	¼yd (25cm)
Teal	GP19-TE:	¼yd (25cm)

PAPERWEIGHT
Cobalt	GP20-CB:	¼yd (25cm)
Pastel	GP20-PT:	¼yd (25cm)
Sludge	GP20-SL:	¼yd (25cm)

ORGANIC STRIPE
Green	GP21-GN:	⅜yd (35cm) or ⅝yd (60cm) if fussy cutting.
Pink	GP21-PK:	⅜yd (35cm)

SWIGGLE
Pink	GP22-PK:	½yd (45cm)

BLUE AND WHITE STRIPE
	BWS 02:	¼yd (25cm)

DOUBLE IKAT CHECKERBOARD
Magenta	DiC 02:	¼yd (25cm)

DOUBLE IKAT POLKA
Sage	DiP 01:	⅜yd (35cm)
Scarlet	DiP 03:	⅜yd (35cm)
Blue	DiP 05:	⅜yd (35cm)

OMBRE STRIPE
	OS 02:	¼yd (25cm)
	OS 05:	¼yd (25cm)

SHOT COTTON
Opal	SC 05:	¼yd (25cm)
Raspberry	SC 08:	¼yd (25cm)
Watermelon	SC 33:	¼yd (25cm)
Sunshine	SC 35:	¼yd (25cm)
Lilac	SC 36:	¼yd (25cm)

Backing Fabric:
ORGANIC STRIPE
Pink	GP21-PK:	3⅜yds (3.1m)

Binding Fabric:
Pieced from leftover fabric.

Batting:
60in x 77in (152.5cm x 195.5cm).

Quilting thread:
Toning machine quilting thread.

Templates:
see page 105

Quilt Assembly

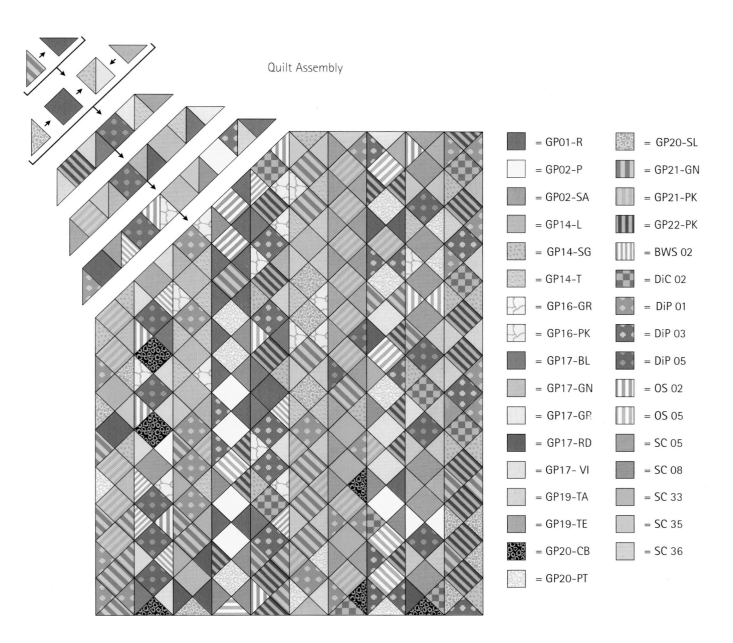

= GP01-R
= GP02-P
= GP02-SA
= GP14-L
= GP14-SG
= GP14-T
= GP16-GR
= GP16-PK
= GP17-BL
= GP17-GN
= GP17-GR
= GP17-RD
= GP17- VI
= GP19-TA
= GP19-TE
= GP20-CB
= GP20-PT

= GP20-SL
= GP21-GN
= GP21-PK
= GP22-PK
= BWS 02
= DiC 02
= DiP 01
= DiP 03
= DiP 05
= OS 02
= OS 05
= SC 05
= SC 08
= SC 33
= SC 35
= SC 36

PATCH SHAPES
This quilt is pieced using a square patch shape (Template X) alternated with squares pieced using a triangle patch shape (Template Y). These blocks are joined in diagonal rows with the ends of the rows completed with more triangle patch shapes (Template Y). The placement of colour gives the impression that the quilt is pieced in vertical columns.

CUTTING OUT
Note: If fussy cutting refer to the photograph for assistance.
Template Y: For Fabrics OS 02 and OS 05

Cut 3³/₈in (8.5cm) wide strips across the width of the fabric. Each strip will give you 11 patches per 45in (114cm) wide fabric. This ensures the correct stripe direction. Cut 7 in OS 02 and 4 in OS 05.
For the remaining fabrics cut 4⁷/₈in (12.5cm) wide strips across the width of the fabric. Each strip will give you 16 patches per 45in (114cm) wide fabric. Cut 17 in GP21-GN, 16 in GP14-SG, DiP 01, SC 36, 14 in GP01-R, GP14-T, 12 in GP02-SA, 11 in GP22-PK, DiP 03, SC 08, 9 in GP16-PK, GP17-RD, GP19-TA, GP19-TE, 8 in GP14-L, GP17-BL, GP17-VI,

GP20-SL, BWS 02, SC 35, 7 in GP16-GR, 6 in GP17-GR, GP20-PT, GP21-PK, 5 in SC 33, 4 in GP17-GN, GP20-CB, 3 in GP02-P, DiC 02, 2 in DiP 05 and 1 in SC 05.
Template X: Cut 4¹/₂in (11.5cm) wide strips across the width of the fabric. Each strip will give you 9 patches per 45in (114cm) wide fabric. Cut 15 in GP21-PK, 12 in GP22-PK, DiP 05, 10 in GP21-GN, 7 in GP17-GN, DiP 01, DiP 03, SC 05, 6 in GP02-P, GP20-PT, DiC 02, 5 in OS 05, 4 in SC 33, 3 in GP17-GR, GP17-RD, GP20-SL, 2 in GP19-TE, GP20-CB, OS 02 and 1 in GP01-R.

Monkey Puzzle Quilt ★★

PAULINE SMITH

Binding: Cut strips 2¹/₂in (6.25cm) wide strips from leftover fabric. Piece into a long strip 7¹/₂yds (6.9m).

Backing: Cut 1 piece 60in x 44in (152.5cm by 112cm) and 1 piece 60in x 34in (152.5cm by 86.5cm) in GP21-PK.

MAKING THE QUILT
Using a ¹/₄in (6mm) seam allowance throughout, piece 117 blocks as shown in the block assembly diagram. Lay out the pieced blocks alternately with the square patch shapes (template X) filling in the row ends with the spare triangle shapes (Template Y) as shown in the quilt assembly diagram. Carefully separate the diagonal rows and stitch. Join the rows to form the quilt.

Block Assembly

FINISHING THE QUILT
Press the quilt top. Seam the backing pieces using a ¹/₄in (6mm) seam allowance to form a piece approx 60in x 77in (152.5cm x 195.5cm). Layer the quilt top, batting and backing and baste together (see page 112). Using a toning machine quilting thread quilt a loose meander pattern as shown in the quilting diagram. Trim the quilt edges and attach the binding (see page 113).

Quilting Diagram

Soft prints in shades of blue, green and pink give this quilt a very English look.

SIZE OF QUILT
The finished quilt will measure approx. 98in x 78in (249cm x 198cm).

MATERIALS
Patchwork Fabrics:

ROMAN GLASS		
Blue and White	GP01-BW:	³/₈yd (35cm)
Pastel	GP01-P:	³/₄yd (70cm)
DAMASK		
Smoky Blue	GP02-SM:	1¹/₄yds (1.2m)
ARTICHOKES		
Circus	GP07-C:	³/₈yd (35cm)
FORGET-ME-NOT ROSE		
Circus	GP08-C:	⁵/₈yd (60cm)
CHRYSANTHEMUM		
Blue	GP13-B:	¹/₄yd (25cm)
Grey	GP13-GR:	⁷/₈yd (80cm)
Ochre	GP13-O:	¹/₄yd (25cm)
DOTTY		
Sea Green	GP14-SG:	⁷/₈yd (80cm)
PEONY		
Blue	GP17-BL:	1¹/₄yds (1.2m)
Violet	GP17-VI:	1¹/₈yds (1.1m)
AUGUST ROSES		
Pastel	GP18-PT:	⁵/₈yd (60cm)
SHOT COTTON		
Ecru	SC 24:	³/₈yd (35cm)
Border Fabric:		
AUGUST ROSES		
Pastel	GP18-PT:	1¹/₄yds (1.2m)
Backing Fabric:		
DAMASK		
Smoky Blue	GP02-SM:	5³/₄yds (5.30m)

Quilt Assembly

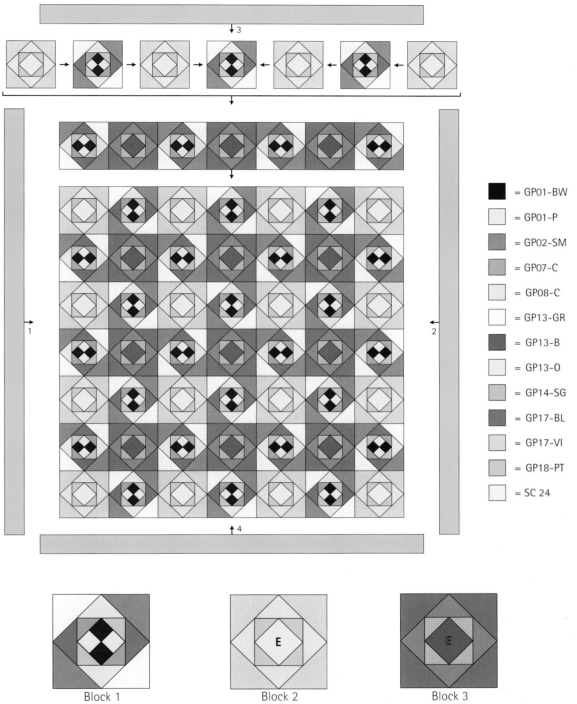

= GP01-BW
= GP01-P
= GP02-SM
= GP07-C
= GP08-C
= GP13-GR
= GP13-B
= GP13-O
= GP14-SG
= GP17-BL
= GP17-VI
= GP18-PT
= SC 24

Block 1

Block 2

Block 3

Binding Fabric:
DOTTY
Sea Green   GP14-SG:
          see patchwork fabrics
Batting:
102in x 82in (259cm x 208cm).
Quilting thread:
Smoky blue hand quilting thread.

Templates:
see pages 99, 103, 106

E   F   G   H   I

PATCH SHAPES
Two square patch shapes (Template E and
F) and three triangle patch shapes
(Template G, H and I) are pieced to make
traditional 'square in a square' blocks.
There are three colourways for the blocks
which combine to make the traditional
Monkey Puzzle design.

73

CUTTING OUT

Note: For fabric GP18-PT which is a large print, sort template G patch shapes into 'mostly pink' for block 2, and use the remaining patches in block 1.

Template E: Cut 4in (10.25cm) wide strips across the width of the fabric. Each strip will give you 11 patches per 45in (114cm) wide fabric. Cut 20 in GP13-O and 12 in GP13-B.

Template F: Cut 2¼in (5.75cm) wide strips across the width of the fabric. Each strip will give you 19 patches per 45in (114cm) wide fabric. Cut 62 in GP01-BW and SC24.

Template G: Cut 3⅜in (8.5cm) wide strips across the width of the fabric. Each strip will give you 26 patches per 45in (114cm) wide fabric. Cut 142 in GP18-PT, 62 in GP07-C and 48 in GP14-SG.

Template H: Cut 4⅜in (11.25cm) wide strips across the width of the fabric. Each strip will give you 18 patches per 45in (114cm) wide fabric. Cut 80 in GP01-P, 62 in GP08-C, GP17-BL and 48 in GP02-SM.

Template I: Cut 5⅞in (15cm) wide strips across the width of the fabric. Each strip will give you 14 patches per 45in (114cm) wide fabric. Cut 80 in GP17-VI, 62 in GP02-SM, GP13-GR and 48 in GP17-BL.

Borders: Cut 9 strips 4½in (11.5cm) wide x width of fabric in GP18-PT.

Binding: Cut 9 strips 2½in (6.25cm) wide x width of fabric in GP14-SG.

Block Assembly

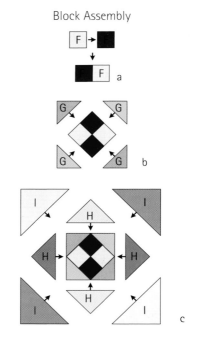

Backing: Cut 1 piece 102in x 45in (259cm by 114cm) and 1 piece 102in x 38in (259cm by 96.5cm) in GP02-SM.

MAKING THE QUILT

Using a ¼in (6mm) seam allowance throughout, piece 31 of block 1 as shown in block assembly diagrams a, b and c. For blocks 2 and 3 replace the centre pieced 4 patch block with a template E patch. Piece 20 of block 2 and 12 of block 3. Lay out the blocks referring to the quilt assembly diagram for block placement and direction, the orientation of block 1 alternates in each row. Join the blocks into 9 rows of 7 blocks. Join the rows to form the quilt centre.

ADDING THE BORDERS

Join the border strips as necessary and cut 2 borders each 90½in x 4½in (230cm x11.5cm) for the quilt sides and 2 borders each 78½in x 4½in (199.5cm x 11.5cm) for the quilt top and bottom. Add the borders to the quilt centre in the order indicated by the quilt assembly diagram.

FINISHING THE QUILT

Press the quilt top. Seam the backing pieces using a ¼in (6mm) seam allowance to form a piece approx. 102in x 82in (259cm x 208cm). Layer the quilt top, batting and backing and baste together (see page 112). Using a smoky blue quilting thread, hand quilt the design shown in the quilting diagram. Trim the quilt edges and attach the binding (see page 113).

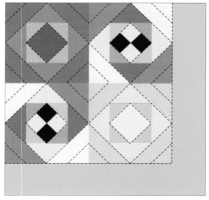

Quilting Diagram

Pastel Gridlock Quilt ★

LIZA PRIOR LUCY

This quilt can be made in any wonderful combinations of colour. The materials listed are those Liza chose but they are only a suggestion to get your creative juices flowing. The instructions for this quilt are more informal than usual. However, we have drawn Liza's quilt accurately to help you with your colour and fabric selection.

SIZE OF QUILT
The finished quilt will measure approx. 68in x 80in (173cm x 203cm).

MATERIALS
Patchwork Fabrics:
Note: Buy ¹/₂yd (45cm) in the dominant 'feature' fabrics and ¹/₄yd (25cm) of the fabrics you will use occasionally. If you add stripes to your palette you will need to buy ¹/₂yd (45cm) for the stripes to run horizontally in block 1.

DAMASK		
Pastel	GP02-P:	¹/₄yd (25cm)
PEONY		
Violet	GP17-VI:	⁷/₈yd (80cm)
includes binding.		
FRUIT BASKET		
Apricot	GP19-AP:	¹/₄yd (25cm)
Taupe	GP19-TA:	¹/₄yd (25cm)
PAPERWEIGHT		
Pastel	GP20-PT:	¹/₄yd (25cm)
ORGANIC STRIPE		
Blue	GP21-BL:	¹/₄yd (25cm)
Green	GP21-GN:	¹/₄yd (25cm)
Lime	GP21-LM:	¹/₄yd (25cm)
Pink	GP21-PK:	¹/₄yd (25cm)
SWIGGLE		
Ochre	GP22-OC:	¹/₄yd (25cm)
SINGLE IKAT WASH		
Peach	SiW 01:	¹/₂yd (45cm)
Banana	SiW 03:	¹/₂yd (45cm)
Green	SiW 04:	¹/₂yd (45cm)
Lavender	SiW 05:	¹/₂yd (45cm)
SHOT COTTON		
Tangerine	SC 11:	¹/₄yd (25cm)
Lavender	SC 14:	¹/₄yd (25cm)
Lichen	SC 19:	¹/₄yd (25cm)
Ecru	SC 24:	¹/₄yd (25cm)
Blush	SC 28:	¹/₄yd (25cm)
Mushroom	SC 31:	¹/₄yd (25cm)
Rosy	SC 32:	¹/₄yd (25cm)
Watermelon	SC 33:	¹/₄yd (25cm)
Sunshine	SC 35:	¹/₄yd (25cm)
Lilac	SC 36:	¹/₄yd (25cm)
Biscuit	SC 38:	¹/₄yd (25cm)
Apple	SC 39:	¹/₄yd (25cm)
Lime	SC 43:	¹/₄yd (25cm)

Backing Fabric:
SHOT COTTON
Apple	SC 39: 4yds (3.7m)

Binding Fabric:
PEONY
Violet	GP17-VI: see patchwork fabrics.

Batting:
72in x 84in (183cm x 213cm)

Quilting thread:
Machine quilting thread in a selection of colours.

Templates:
see pages 99, 105

RR   AA

PATCH SHAPES
A large square patch shape (Template RR) is used for the pieced border and the centre of block 1. Block 1 is completed using strips of random width. Block 2 is a 6 x 6 checkerboard block pieced using a small square patch shape (Template AA). The blocks are alternated throughout the quilt.

Quilt Assembly

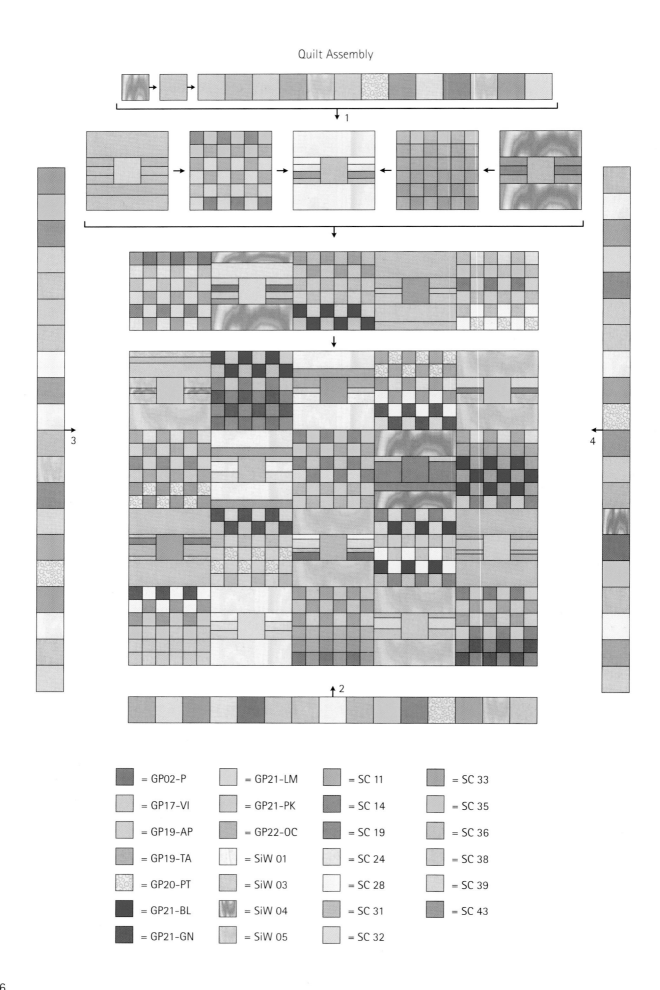

■ = GP02-P	☐ = GP21-LM	■ = SC 11	■ = SC 33
☐ = GP17-VI	■ = GP21-PK	■ = SC 14	■ = SC 35
☐ = GP19-AP	■ = GP22-OC	■ = SC 19	■ = SC 36
■ = GP19-TA	☐ = SiW 01	☐ = SC 24	■ = SC 38
▦ = GP20-PT	■ = SiW 03	☐ = SC 28	☐ = SC 39
■ = GP21-BL	▨ = SiW 04	■ = SC 31	■ = SC 43
■ = GP21-GN	▦ = SiW 05	☐ = SC 32	

CUTTING OUT

Refer to the diagram and photograph for guidance with fabric placement. You will see that Liza chose the Single Ikat Wash fabrics as her dominant 'feature' fabrics, which she also included in the borders.

Template RR: Cut 4½in (11.5cm) wide strips across the width of the fabric. Each strip will give you 9 patches per 45in (114cm) wide fabric. Cut a total of 85 in a random colour selection. The Shot Cottons look good as centres to block 1.

Template AA: Cut 2½in (6.5cm) wide strips across the width of the fabric. Each strip will give you 17 patches per 45in (114cm) wide fabric. Split your fabrics into lighter and darker shades and cut 270 in lighter fabrics and 270 in darker fabrics. Total 540 squares.

Strips for Block 1: Cut these as you are piecing the blocks.

Binding: Cut 8 strips 2½in (6.25cm) wide x width of fabric in GP17-VI.

Backing: Cut 2 pieces 72in x 42.5in (183cm x 108cm) in SC 39.

MAKING THE BLOCKS

Use ¼in (6mm) seam allowance throughout. Refer to the diagram and photograph for guidance with fabric placement.

For Block 1, select one of your dominant 'feature' fabrics for the background. Select a contrasting large square for the block centre, then choose related tones for the accent colour strips. Cut strips of random width and join to make 2 pieces 4½in x 12½in (11.5cm x 31.75cm) for the block top and bottom, or use a single piece of the feature fabric without piecing. Then make 1 piece 4½in x 9in (11.5cm x 23cm) using 2, 3 or 4 strips. Cut this in half to make 2 pieces 4½in x 4½in (11.5cm x 11.5cm) for the block sides. Join these to the sides of the centre square and then add the top and bottom strips to complete the block as shown in the block 1 assembly diagram. Make a total of 15 blocks.

For Block 2, arrange 18 lighter squares and 18 darker squares alternately into 6 rows of 6 squares, using the same 2 colours in each horizontal row and the same 2 colours for 1-4 rows. Join the rows as shown in the block 2 assembly diagram. Make a total of 15 blocks.

MAKING THE QUILT

Lay out the blocks alternately into 6 rows of 5 blocks, Join the blocks into rows, join the rows to make the quilt centre.

ADDING THE BORDERS

Piece the borders as shown in the quilt assembly diagram and join to the quilt centre in the order indicted.

FINISHING THE QUILT

Press the quilt top. Seam the backing pieces using a ¼in (6mm) seam allowance to form a piece approx. 72in x 84in (183cm x 213cm). Layer the quilt top, batting and backing and baste together (see page 112). Liza's quilt was quilted with concentric squares and rectangles which is hard to achieve on a domestic sewing machine, so she suggests using a meander or stipple pattern for the background of block 1 and a squared spiral for the centre of the block, as shown in the quilting diagram and on block 2 quilt in the ditch along the seam lines. Trim the quilt edges and attach the binding (see page 113).

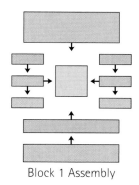

Block 1 Assembly

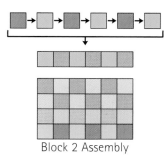

Block 2 Assembly

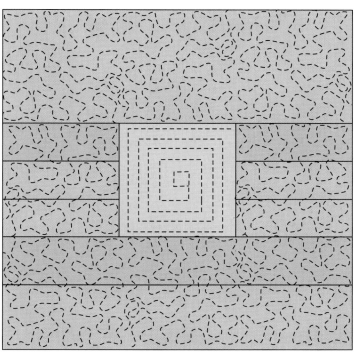

Quilting Diagram

Sophisticated Play Quilt ★ ★

Mary Mashuta

Mary loves to add lots of colours and a sense of whimsy to her quilts. Kaffe's fabrics make that easy.

SIZE OF QUILT
The finished quilt will measure approx. 48in x 55½in (122cm x 141cm).

MATERIALS
Patchwork Fabrics:
BROAD CHECK

BC 01: 1⅝yds (1.5m) includes bias binding

BROAD STRIPE

BS 06: 1¾yds (1.6m)

SHOT COTTON
Ginger	SC 01: ¼yd (25cm)
Cassis	SC 02: ¼yd (25cm)
Opal	SC 05: ⅛yd (15cm)
Raspberry	SC 08: ⅛yd (15cm)
Bittersweet	SC 10: ⅛yd (15cm)
Denim	SC 15: ⅛yd (15cm)
Sage	SC 17: ⅛yd (15cm)
Tobacco	SC 18: ⅛yd (15cm)
Pine	SC 21: ⅛yd (15cm)
Pewter	SC 22: ¼yd (25cm)
Charcoal	SC 25: ⅜yd (35cm)
Grass	SC 27: ¼yd (25cm)
Mushroom	SC 31: ⅛yd (15cm)
Watermelon	SC 33: ⅛yd (15cm)
Apple	SC 39: ⅛yd (15cm)

Backing Fabric:
PAPERWEIGHT

Sludge   GP20-SL: 2¼yds (2.1m)

Bias Binding:
BROAD CHECK

BC 01:
See patchwork fabrics

Batting:
52in x 60in (132cm x 152.5cm).
Quilting thread:
Toning machine quilting thread.

Templates:
see pages 103, 104, 106

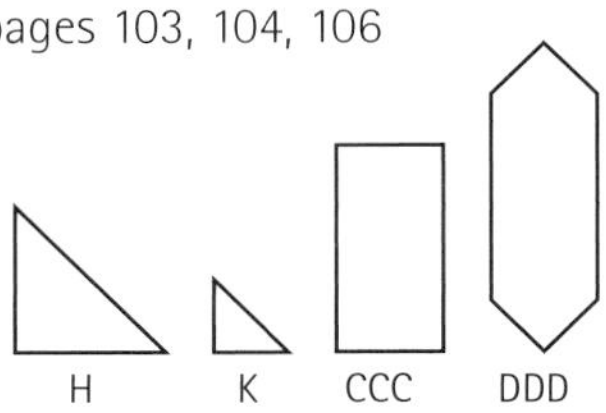

H   K   CCC   DDD

PATCH SHAPES
The quilt centre is made from hourglass blocks pieced using a large triangle patch shape (Templates H). The blocks are interspaced with a rectangle patch shape (Template CCC) and stitched into rows. These rows are alternated with a second row comprised of 1 lozenge patch shape (Template DDD) and 1 small triangle patch shape (Template K). Each hourglass block is embellished with a large Suffolk Puff.

CUTTING OUT
Template CCC: Cut 3in (7.75cm) wide strips across the width of the fabric. Each strip will give you 7 patches per 45in (114cm) wide fabric. Cut 49 in BS 06.
Template DDD: Cut 3in (7.75cm) wide strips across the width of the fabric. Each strip will give you 5 patches per 45in (114cm) wide fabric. Cut 48 in BS 06.
Template K: Cut 2⅝in (6.75cm) wide strips across the width of the fabric. Each strip will give you 32 patches per 45in (114cm) wide fabric. Cut 112 in SC 25. Also cut 16 in BS 06, these can be cut from the leftover fabric from templates CCC and DDD. Note: the stripe direction should be aligned with the long side of the triangle, refer to the quilt assembly diagram for guidance.
Template H: Cut 3⅛in (8cm) wide strips across the width of the fabric. Each strip will give you 12 patches per 45in (114cm) wide fabric. Cut 18 in SC 01, SC 02, SC 22, SC 27, 12 in SC 05 SC 08, SC 10, SC 15, SC 18, SC 21, 6 in SC 17, SC 31, SC 33 and SC 39.
Suffolk Puffs: Cut 42 circles 5⅜in (13.75cm) in diameter in BC 01.

Quilt Assembly

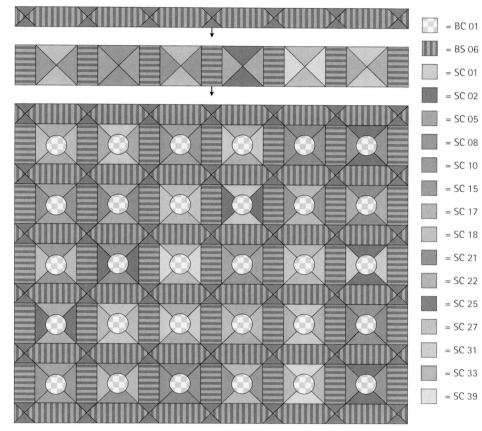

Row 1

Row 2

= BC 01
= BS 06
= SC 01
= SC 02
= SC 05
= SC 08
= SC 10
= SC 15
= SC 17
= SC 18
= SC 21
= SC 22
= SC 25
= SC 27
= SC 31
= SC 33
= SC 39

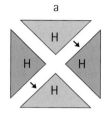

a

Block Assembly

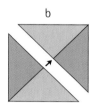

b

Backing: Cut 1 piece 60in x 44in (152.5cm x 112cm) and 2 pieces 30¹/₂in x 9in (77.5cm x 23cm) in GP20-SL.

Binding: Cut 6¹/₄yds (5.7m) of 2¹/₂in- (6.5cm-) wide bias binding in BC 01.

MAKING THE BLOCKS
Using a ¹/₄in (6mm) seam allowance throughout and referring to the quilt assembly diagram for fabric combinations, make up 42 hourglass blocks, using block assembly diagram a and b as a guide.

MAKING THE ROWS
Row 1: Arrange the template CCC lozenge shapes interspaced with the template K triangles and stitch as shown in the quilt

assembly diagram filling in the ends with additional template K triangles.
Make 8 rows.
Row 2: Take the pieced hourglass blocks and interspace with the template DDD rectangles and stitch. Make 7 rows.

MAKING THE QUILT
Arrange the rows alternately and matching the intersections carefully join the rows to form the quilt top as shown in the quilt assembly diagram.

MAKING THE SUFFOLK PUFFS
Turn under a ¹/₄in (6mm) hem on each fabric circle and sew a running stitch using strong thread around the outer edge. Making sure the right side of the fabric is the outside of the Puff, gently

pull the thread, gathering the fabric until a small opening is left. Knot the thread. Make 42. Put to one side until after the quilting is complete.

FINISHING THE QUILT
Press the quilt top. Seam the backing pieces using a ¹/₄in (6mm) seam allowance to form a piece approx. 52in x 60in (132cm x 152.5cm). Layer the quilt top, batting and backing and baste together (see page 112). Machine quilt in the ditch around all the shapes except the diagonals of the hourglass blocks. Quilt a wiggly line along both diagonal seams of the hourglass blocks. Stitch a Suffolk puff at the centre of each hourglass block. Trim the quilt edges and attach the binding (see page 113).

Wheel Of Fortune Quilt ★ ★ ★

Kaffe Fassett

A fairly common Star layout but my contrasting palette made me think of casinos and Baccarat tables. The instructions given are for the English paper piecing method, the easiest way to piece this quilt.

SIZE OF QUILT
The finished quilt will measure approx.
61¹/₂in x 61¹/₂in (156cm x 156cm).

MATERIALS
Patchwork Fabrics:
BUBBLES
Plum   GP15-P: ¹/₄yd (25cm)
PEONY
Maroon   GP17-MR: 1 yd (90cm)
FRUIT BASKET
Black   GP19-BK: ⁵/₈yd (60cm)
              or use leftover from backing
Teal   GP19-TE: ³/₄yd (70cm)
DOUBLE IKAT CHECKERBOARD
Magenta   DiC 02: ¹/₈yd (15cm)
Indigo   DiC 03: ¹/₈yd (15cm)
Gold   DiC 04: ¹/₈yd (15cm)
Swede   DiC 05: ¹/₂yd (45cm)
DOUBLE IKAT POLKA
Scarlet   DiP 03: ¹/₂yd (45cm)
Denim   DiP 04: ¹/₂yd (45cm)
Blue   DiP 05: ¹/₄yd (25cm)

Navy   DiP 06: ¹/₄yd (25cm)
PACHRANGI STRIPE
              PS 05: ¹/₂yd (45cm)
SHOT COTTON
Pomegranate   SC 09: ¹/₂yd (45cm)
Backing Fabric:
FRUIT BASKET
Black   GP19-BK: 3³/₄yds (3.4m)
Binding Fabric:
PEONY
Maroon   GP17-MR: see
              patchwork fabrics

Batting:
66in x 66in (167.5cm x 167.5cm).
Quilting thread:
Perle cotton thread in burnt orange.

Templates:
see pages 100, 104

L   M   N

PATCH SHAPES

This variation on a 'tumbling blocks' theme is pieced using a square patch shape (Template L) and a diamond patch shape (Template M). Extra squares are added to complete the quilt into a square shape and a further triangular patch shape (Template N) is used to fill in on the extreme edges of the quilt sides. As there are so many inset seams in this quilt it is best suited to hand piecing.

CUTTING OUT

Template L: Cut 3¹/₂in (9cm) wide strips across the width of the fabric. Each strip will give you 12 patches per 45in (114cm) wide fabric. Cut 40 in DiP 04, 24 in DiC 05, DiP 05, PS 05, 20 in GP15-P, 16 in SC 09, 12 in DiC 02, DiC 04, DiP 06, 8 in GP17-MR, DiC 03 and 4 in GP19-TE.
Template M: Cut 2⁵/₈in (6.75cm) wide strips across the width of the fabric. Each strip will give you 10 patches per 45in (114cm) wide fabric. Cut 72 in GP19-BK, 64 in GP19-TE, 56 in DiP 03, 48 in GP17-MR, 28 in SC 09, 12 in PS 05 and 8 in DiP 06.
Template N: Cut 3⁷/₈in (10cm) wide strips across the width of the fabric. Each strip will give you 22 patches per 45in (114cm) wide fabric. Cut 24 in DiC 05.

Binding: Cut 6 strips 2¹/₂in (6.25cm) wide x width of fabric in GP17-MR.

Backing: Cut 1 piece 66in x 44in (167.5cm by 112cm) and 1 piece 66in x 23in (167.5cm by 58.5cm) in GP19-BK.

MAKING THE QUILT

This quilt is made in segments, make 4 of each of the segment type (Segments 1 and 2) to complete the quilt referring carefully to the quilt assembly diagram for fabric placement. Using the 'English' hand piecing method (see page 110) piece together blocks as shown in block assembly diagrams a and b. Diagram c shows how to complete the first row of segment 1. Complete the other rows for segment 1 and piece the rows together. Make 4. Piece segment 2 in the same manner. Make 4. Join the segments to form the quilt as indicated on the quilt assembly diagram. Note: Do not remove papers until a patch shape is completely enclosed by other patches on all sides.

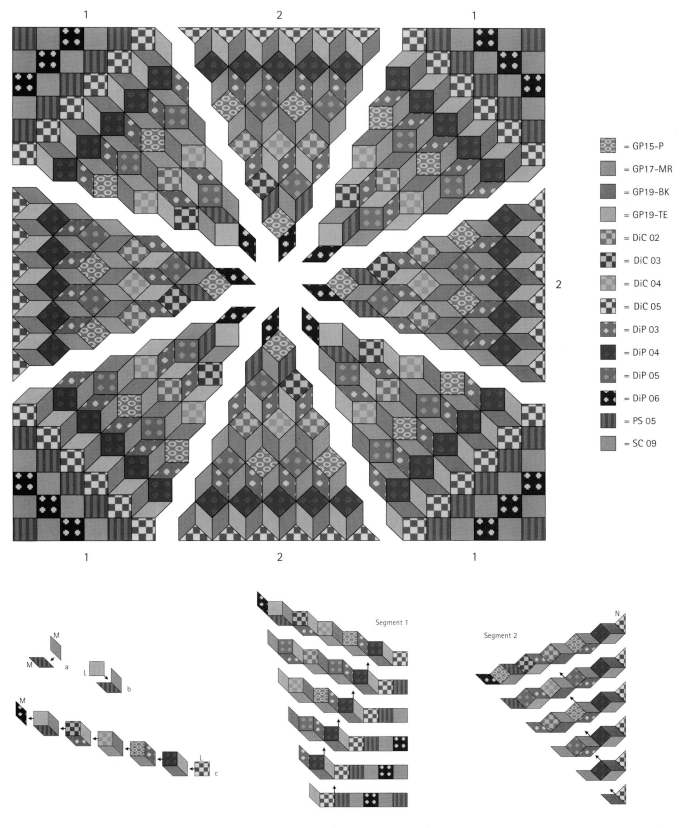

1　　　　　2　　　　　1

2　　　　　　　　　　　　　　2

1　　　　　2　　　　　1

= GP15-P

= GP17-MR

= GP19-BK

= GP19-TE

= DiC 02

= DiC 03

= DiC 04

= DiC 05

= DiP 03

= DiP 04

= DiP 05

= DiP 06

= PS 05

= SC 09

Segment 1

Segment 2

N

FINISHING THE QUILT
Remove any remaining papers and press the
quilt top. Seam the backing pieces using a
1/4in (6mm) seam allowance to form a piece

approx. 66in x 66in (167.5cm x 167.5cm).
Layer the quilt top, batting and backing and
baste together (see page 112). Using a burnt
orange perle cotton thread, working from

the centre out hand quilt concentric circles.
The photograph on page 26 shows this
beautifully. Trim the quilt edges and attach
the binding (see page 113).

Cinque De Mayo Quilt ★ ★

SANDY DONABED

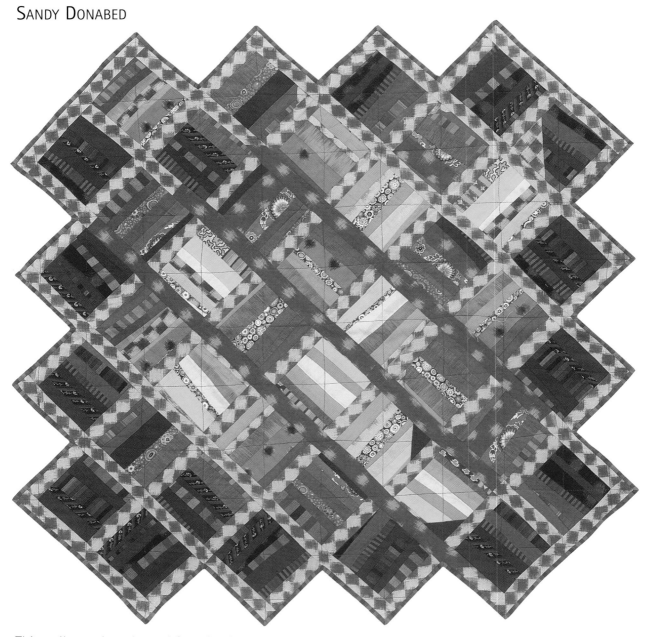

This quilt can be adapted for a beginner or experienced quilter alike. You can scale the block size or make more or less blocks, and arrange them as you please. As pictured it makes a great unconventional baby quilt or table topper. Sandy's freehand foundation piecing method is easy and quick, so your quilt should be finished in no time.

SIZE OF QUILT
The finished quilt will measure approx.
51in x 51in (130cm x 130cm).

MATERIALS
Patchwork Fabrics:
ROMAN GLASS
Red   GP01-R: ¹/₈yd (15cm)
PAPERWEIGHT
Pumpkin   GP20-PN: ¹/₈yd (15cm)

DIAGONAL POPPY
Aubergine   GP24-AU: ¹/₈yd (15cm)
PAISLEY
Raspberry   GP27-RS: ¹/₈yd (15cm)
BROAD STRIPE
             BS 08: ¹/₈yd (15cm)
EXOTIC STRIPE
             ES 10: ¹/₈yd (15cm)
DOUBLE IKAT CHECKERBOARD
Scarlet   DiC 01: ³/₄yd (70cm)

Magenta   DiC 02: ¹/₈yd (15cm)
DOUBLE IKAT POLKA
Pumpkin   DiP 02: ¹/₈yd (15cm)
             or use leftover
             from backing
Scarlet   DiP 03: ¹/₄yd (25cm)
Denim   DiP 04: ¹/₈yd (15cm)
NARROW STRIPE
             NS 01: ¹/₂yd (45cm)
             NS 09: ¹/₈yd (15cm)

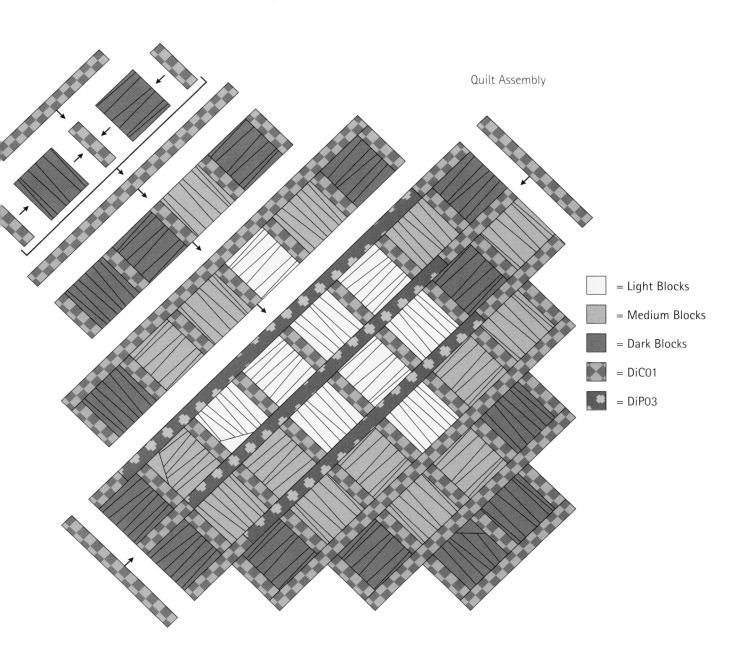

Quilt Assembly

☐ = Light Blocks

▨ = Medium Blocks

▨ = Dark Blocks

▨ = DiC01

▨ = DiP03

PACHRANGI STRIPE
            PS 05: ¹⁄₈yd (15cm)

SINGLE IKAT WASH
Red   SiW 06: ¹⁄₈yd (15cm)
SHOT COTTON
Ginger   SC 01: ¹⁄₈yd (15cm)
Cassis   SC 02: ¹⁄₄yd (25cm)
Raspberry   SC 08: ¹⁄₈yd (15cm)
Pomegranate   SC 09: ¹⁄₈yd (15cm)
Bittersweet   SC 10: ¹⁄₈ yd (15cm)
Tangerine   SC 11: ¹⁄₈yd (15cm)
Watermelon   SC 33: ¹⁄₈yd (15cm)
Lemon   SC 34: ¹⁄₈yd (15cm)
Sunshine   SC 35: ¹⁄₈yd (15cm)
Scarlet   SC 44: ¹⁄₈yd (15cm)

Backing Fabric:
DOUBLE IKAT POLKA
Pumpkin   DiP 02: 2¹⁄₄yds (2.1m)
Binding Fabric:
NARROW STRIPE
                 NS 01:
                 See patchwork fabrics

Batting:
55in x 55in (140cm x 140cm).

Quilting thread:
Toning machine quilting thread.

PATCH SHAPES
6in (15.25cm) square foundation papers
are used for the blocks, which are

interspaced with sashing strips cut at
2in (5cm) wide.

CUTTING OUT
The fabrics are sorted into three colour
groups as follows:
Darks - red/maroon:
GP24-AU, BS 08, DiP 04, NS 09, PS 05,
SC 01, SC 02, SC 09 and SC10.
Mediums - orange/deep golds
GP01-R, GP20-PN, GP27-RS, DiC 02,
DiP 02, DiP 03, ES 10, NS 01, SiW 06,
SC 08, SC 10 and SC 11.
Lights - yellow/pink
GP20-PN, GP22-PK, DiC 02, SC 11, SC 33,
SC 34 and SC 35.

Block Diagrams

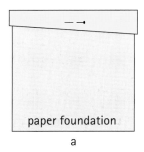 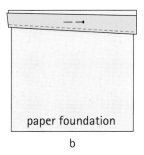 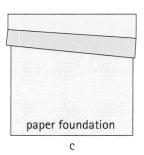

a　　　　　　　　　　b　　　　　　　　　　c

Cut several strips from each fabric, varying in width from about 1in (2.5cm) up to 3in (7.5cm). Sandy made a point of making the strips irregular, cutting most thin at one end and wide at the other. Next sort the strips into 3 bags, marked Dark, Medium and Light, this keeps them contained at the sewing machine and helps to keep the selection process random.

Sashing:
Cut 2in (5cm) wide strips in DiC 01 and DiP 03. Sandy cut some of the sashing on the bias so the checked fabric looks like little pieced squares, but if you are a beginner cut the sashing on the straight grain, it is much easier to work with. Joining the strips where necessary, cut a total of 44 sashing strips 6in x 2in (15.25 x 5cm), 4 sashing strips 16in x 2in (40.5 x 5cm), 2 sashing strips 30in x 2in (76cm x 5cm), 2 sashing strips 44in x 2in (112cm x 5cm), and 3 sashing strips 55in x 2in (140cm x 5cm).

Backing: Cut 1 piece 55in x 45in (140cm x 114cm), 1 piece 45in x 12in (114cm x 30.5cm) and 1 piece 12in x 11in (30.5cm x 28cm) in DiP 02.

Binding: Cut 6 strips 2½in (6.5cm) wide x width of fabric in NS 01.

MAKING THE BLOCKS
Cut 40 foundation papers 6in (15.25cm) square from thin paper. Set the sewing machine stitch length very short, to make tearing the papers easier. Starting with the 'Darks' fabric bag pull out a strip, place right side up along the top of the foundation paper slightly overlapping the paper edge and pin as shown in block diagram a. Take another strip and place on the first strip right sides together, matching the lower edge as shown in diagram b. Stitch through the fabric and paper as shown. Fold the second strip out and press, as shown in diagram c. Repeat the process until all the paper is covered. Sandy also added a corner section to a few of the blocks for added interest. To do this just use a slightly larger strip and place at about 45 degrees across the corner and stitch in place, fold back to form a triangle. Trim away any strips from beneath the triangle to reduce bulk.

Sandy recommends working on several blocks at a time to make the sewing process go very fast, she also says "try not to have any of the blocks the same, but don't obsess about it, just reach into the bag and use whatever new strip turns up".

Use about ⅓ of the foundation papers for each of the Dark, Medium and Light fabrics, but again, don't worry if you end up with

more dark than medium or light blocks. If you have more dark blocks the light ones will absolutely sparkle against them, if you end up with many medium blocks the look will be less dynamic and easier to live with.

Trim all the blocks to exactly the paper size.

MAKING THE QUILT
Assemble the blocks into diagonal rows, interspacing the blocks with sashing strips as shown in the quilt assembly diagram. Join the rows and finally add the 4 sashing strips 16in x 2in (40.5 x 5cm) to the corners to complete the quilt top. Remove the foundation papers.

FINISHING THE QUILT
Press the quilt top. Seam the backing pieces using a ¼in (6mm) seam allowance to form a piece approx. 55in x 55in (140cm x 140cm). Layer the quilt top, batting and backing and baste together (see page 112). Using a toning machine quilting thread, stitch a simple diagonal pattern across the surface of the quilt. Trim the quilt edges and attach the binding (see page 113). For the 'inside' corners of the binding stitch up to the corner turning point leaving the needle in the down position, turn the quilt and continue along the next edge. Fold the corner into a mitre and slipstitch in place as usual.

Sky Blue Pink Quilt ★★★

KAFFE FASSETT

I was looking through a book of vintage English quilts when this layout hit me. Recreating it in my fabrics was a pure delight.

SIZE OF QUILT
The finished quilt will measure approx. 73in x 73in (185.5cm x 185.5cm).

MATERIALS
Patchwork Fabrics:
ROMAN GLASS
Pink   GP01-PK: ⁷/₈yd (80cm)
includes binding
ARTICHOKES
Jewel   GP07-J: ¹/₈yd (15cm)
Pastel   GP07-P: ¹/₄yd (25cm)
FORGET-ME-NOT ROSE
Circus   GP08-C: ¹/₄yd (25cm)
FLOWER LATTICE
Pastel   GP11-P: ³/₈yd (35cm)
PEONY
Blue   GP17-BL: ³/₈yd (35cm)
Red   GP17-RD: 1 yd (90cm)
Violet   GP17-VI: ¹/₄yd (25cm)

AUGUST ROSES
Pastel   GP18-PT: ³/₈yd (35cm)
or use leftovers from backing.
FRUIT BASKET
Taupe   GP19-TA: ¹/₄yd (25cm)
ORGANIC STRIPE
Pink   GP21-PK: ⁵/₈yd (60cm)
SWIGGLE
Pink   GP22-PK: 2¹/₄yd (2.1m)
DOUBLE IKAT POLKA
Sage   DiP 01: ¹/₄yd (25cm)
ROWAN STRIPE
      RS 04: ¹/₈yd (15cm)
      RS 05: ¹/₄yd (25cm)
      RS 06: ¹/₄yd (25cm)
SINGLE IKAT WASH
Peach   SiW 01: ¹/₂yd (45cm)
Backing Fabric:
AUGUST ROSES
Pastel   GP18-PT: 4 ³/₈yds (4m)

Binding Fabric:
ROMAN GLASS
Pink   GP01-PK: see
                 patchwork fabrics
Batting:
77in x 77in (196cm x 196cm).
Quilting thread:
Toning machine quilting thread.

Templates:
see pages 99, 100, 102, 106

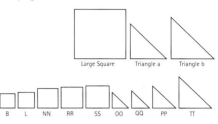

PATCH SHAPES
The quilt is formed by a large central block surrounded by 7 borders - 4 simple with corner posts and 3 pieced. The central square patch shape is cut to 10in (25.5cm), this is surrounded by triangles (triangle a) cut to size. Then comes the first simple border with square corner posts (Template B). The first pieced border is made from triangle patch shapes (Template QQ) pieced into sections and added, followed by more triangles (Triangle b) cut to size. The second simple border with square corner posts (Template NN) is then added. The second pieced border is made with 1 square patch shape (Template L) and 1 triangle patch shape (Template OO), the ends of this section are pieced slightly oversized and are trimmed to fit exactly. This is followed by the third simple border with square corner posts (Template RR). The third pieced border is made up of 1 square patch shape (Template L) pieced into 4 patch blocks and 2 triangle patch shapes (Templates PP and TT). The quilt is finished with a fourth simple border.

CUTTING OUT
Note: Kaffe chose to 'fussy cut' the Swiggle fabric which has 4 different design elements across the width. The diagrams are numbered 1-4 to represent the 4 elements, refer to the diagrams and photograph for placement.
Template B: Cut 3¹/₄in (8.25cm) wide strips. Cut 4 in GP17-VI.

Template L: Cut 3¹/₂in (9cm) wide strips across the width of the fabric. Each strip will give you 12 patches per 45in (114cm) wide fabric. Cut 20 in GP01-PK, 16 in GP18-PT, 13 in GP17-VI, 12 in GP08-C, DiP 01, 11 in GP17-RD, 10 in GP17-BL, GP22-PK Design Element 4, 9 in GP11-P, 6 in GP19-TA, 5 in GP07-P, RS 06, 4 in GP07-J, GP22-PK Design Element 3, RS 05 and 3 in GP21-PK.

Template NN: Cut 4¹/₄in (10.75cm) wide strips. Cut 4 in GP08-C.

Template OO: Cut 2³/₄in (7cm) wide strips across the width of the fabric. Each strip will give you 14 patches per 45in (114cm) wide fabric. Cut 13 in GP19-TA, RS 05, 10 in GP17-BL, RS 06, 7 in DiP 01, 3 in GP07-J, GP22-PK Design Element 1, GP22-PK Design Element 3, GP22-PK Design Element 4, RS 04, 2 in GP08-C and 1 in GP01-PK.

Template PP: Cut 5¹/₈in (13cm) wide strips across the width of the fabric. Each strip will give you 16 patches per 45in (114cm) wide fabric. Cut 32 in GP22-PK Design Element 2.

Template QQ: Cut 3in (7.75cm) wide strips across the width of the fabric. Each strip will give you 13 patches per 45in (114cm) wide fabric. Cut 5 in GP19-TA, 4 in GP17-BL, RS 05, RS 06, 3 in GP01-PK, RS 04, 2 in GP07-P, GP08-C and 1 on DiP 01.

Template RR: Cut 4¹/₂in (11.5cm) wide strips. Cut 4 in GP11-P.

Template SS: Cut 4³/₄in (12cm) wide strips. Cut 4 in GP17-VI.

Template TT: Cut 4⁷/₈in (12.5cm) wide strips across the width of the fabric. Each strip will give you 7 patches per 45in (114cm) wide fabric. Cut 24 GP22-PK Design Element 1 and 16 in GP22-PK Design Element 2.

Large Square: Cut 1 square 10in x 10in (25.5cm x 25.5cm) in GP18-PT.

Triangle a: Cut 2 squares 7⁵/₈in x 7⁵/₈in (19.5cm x 19.5cm) in GP07-P. Cut each square diagonally to form 2 triangles. Total 4 triangles.

Triangle b: Cut 1 square 7⁷/₈in x 7⁷/₈in (20cm x 20cm) in GP22-PK Design Element 1 and 1 in GP22-PK Design Element 3. Cut each square diagonally to form 2 triangles. Total 4 triangles.

Border 1: Cut 4 strips 13³/₄in x 3in (35cm x 7.75cm) in GP11-P.

Border 2: Cut 4 strips 27in x 4¹/₄in (68.5cm x 10.75cm) in SiW 01.

Border 3: Cut 4 strips 43in x 4in (109.25cm x 10.25cm) in GP21-PK.

Border 4: Cut 7 strips 3¹/₂in (9cm) wide across the width of the fabric in GP17-RD. Join as necessary and cut 2 strips 68in x 3¹/₂in (173cm x 9cm) and 2 strips 74in x 3¹/₂in (188cm x 9cm)

Binding: Cut 8 strips 2¹/₂in (6.25cm) wide x width of fabric in GP01-PK.

Backing: Cut 1 piece 77in x 45in (196cm x 114cm) and 1 piece 77in x 33in (196cm x 84cm) in GP18-PT.

MAKING THE QUILT
Using a ¹/₄in (6mm) seam allowance throughout piece the centre section of the quilt as shown in quilt assembly diagram 1, sub-piecing the sections as shown. The next stage is detailed in quilt assembly diagram 2, again sub-piecing as shown. The pieced sections will be oversized, trim to fit exactly. Once this section is complete, move on to quilt assembly diagram 3. Add border 3, then sub-piece the next layer. Make a total of 28 four patch blocks using the same method as shown for Beaded Curtain Quilt block assembly diagrams a, b and c (see page 58). Piece the four patch blocks with the triangles (templates TT and PP) into borders and add to the quilt centre. Finally add border 4 to complete the quilt.

FINISHING THE QUILT
Press the quilt top. Seam the backing pieces using a ¹/₄in (6mm) seam allowance to form a piece approx. 77in x 77in (196cm x 196cm). Layer the quilt top, batting and backing and baste together (see page 112). Using a toning machine quilting thread stitch-in-the-ditch along the seam lines. Trim the quilt edges and attach the binding (see page 113).

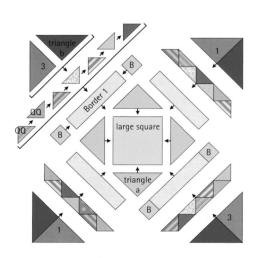

Quilt Assembly 1

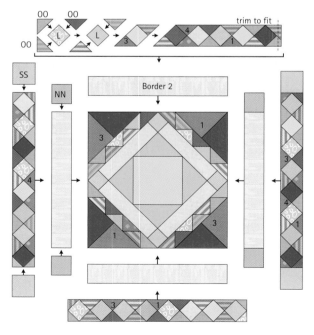

Quilt Assembly 2

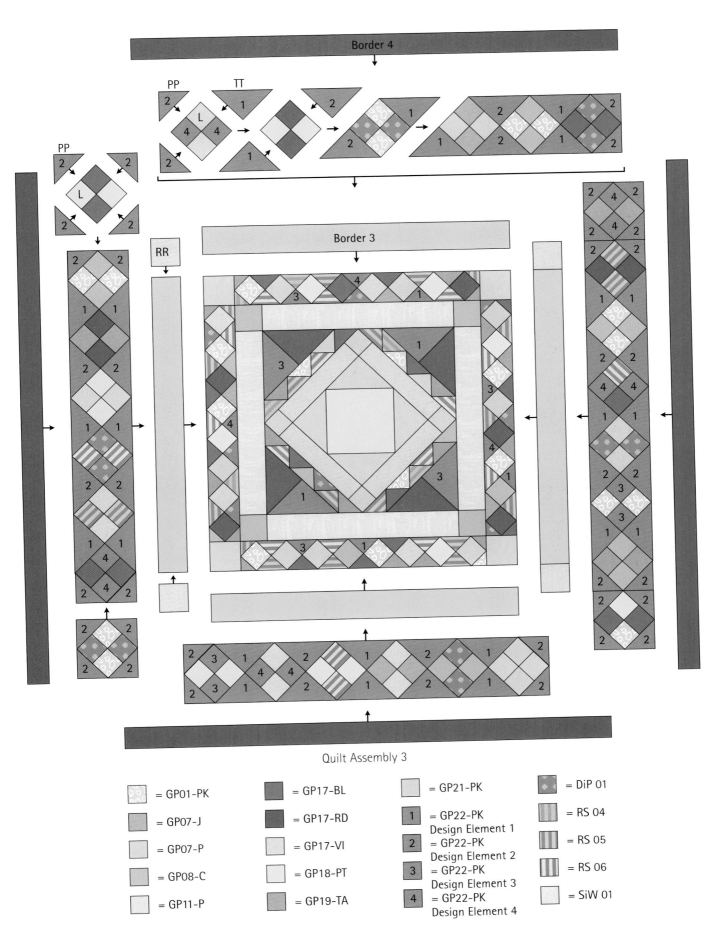

Quilt Assembly 3

= GP01-PK

= GP07-J

= GP07-P

= GP08-C

= GP11-P

= GP17-BL

= GP17-RD

= GP17-VI

= GP18-PT

= GP19-TA

= GP21-PK

1 = GP22-PK
Design Element 1

2 = GP22-PK
Design Element 2

3 = GP22-PK
Design Element 3

4 = GP22-PK
Design Element 4

= DiP 01

= RS 04

= RS 05

= RS 06

= SiW 01

Heather Strippy Quilt ★★

Gill Turley

The mixture of soft heathery colours and subtle quilting on this pretty quilt are simple and stylish.

SIZE OF QUILT
The finished quilt will measure approx. 47¾in x 69½in (121cm x 176.5cm).

MATERIALS
Patchwork Fabrics:
EXOTIC STRIPE

        ES 21: 2yds (1.85m)

NARROW STRIPE

        NS 13: ³/8yd (35cm)

SHOT COTTON
Lavender	SC 14:	⁷/8yd (80cm)
Smoky	SC 20:	³/8yd (35cm)
Lilac	SC 36:	⁵/8yd (60cm)

Backing Fabric:
SINGLE IKAT WASH
Blue	SiW 02:	2⁷/8yds (2.7m)

Bias Binding:
SHOT COTTON
Mushroom	SC 31:	³/4Yd (70cm)

Batting:
51in x 73in (129.5cm x 185.5cm).

Quilting thread:
Toning machine quilting thread and soft lilac and pink cotton à broder no. 16 embroidery thread.

Templates:
see pages 103, 105

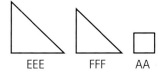

PATCH SHAPES
A small square patch shape (Template AA) is used to piece four patch blocks which are then set on point into vertical rows by the addition of 2 triangle patch shapes (Templates EEE and FFF). The rows are interspaced with cut strips of striped fabric.

CUTTING OUT
Template AA: Cut 2¹/2in (6.5cm) wide strips across the width of the fabric. Each strip will give you 17 patches per 45in (114cm) wide fabric. Cut 72 in NS 13 and SC 20.

Template EEE: Cut 4¹/4in (10.75cm) wide strips across the width of the fabric. Each strip will give you 9 patches per 45in (114cm) wide fabric. Cut 44 in SC 14 and 22 in SC 36.

Template FFF: Cut 5¹/4in (13.5cm) wide strips across the width of the fabric. Each strip will give you 16 patches per 45in (114cm) wide fabric. Cut 8 in SC 14 and 4 in SC 36.

Vertical Strips: Cut 4 strips 7in x 70in (17.75cm x 177.75cm) down the length of the fabric. Note: Gill chose to fussy cut these strips to echo the stripes in each strip. Refer to the photograph for guidance.

Binding: Cut 7yds (6.4m) of 2¹/2in (6.5cm) wide bias binding in SC 31.

Backing: Cut 2 pieces 51in x 37in (129.5cm x 94cm) in SiW 02.

MAKING THE QUILT
Using a ¹/4in (6mm) seam allowance throughout, piece a total of 36 four

Quilt Assembly

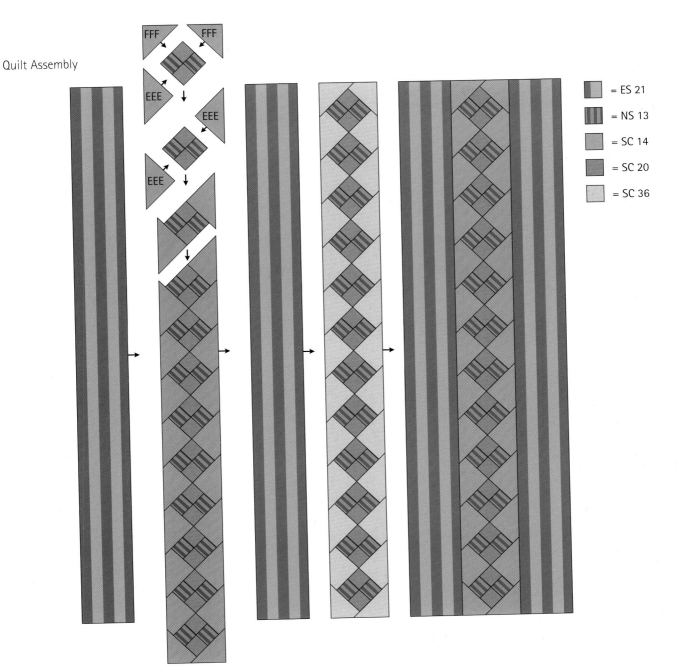

= ES 21

= NS 13

= SC 14

= SC 20

= SC 36

patch blocks using the same method as shown for Beaded Curtain Quilt block assembly diagrams a, b and c (see page 58). Piece these into strips as shown in the quilt assembly diagram using the large template EEE triangles along the sides of the strips, matching the right angle of the triangle with the corner of the four-patch block. The template FFF triangles are added at the top and bottom of the strips, in this case match the centre dot marked on the template with the centre seam of the four-patch block. Make 3 strips referring to the quilt assembly diagram for fabric placement. Alternate the pieced strips with the cut vertical strips and stitch together to form the quilt as shown in the quilt assembly diagram.

FINISHING THE QUILT
Press the quilt top. Seam the backing pieces using a ¹/₄in (6mm) seam allowance to form a piece approx. 51in x 73in (129.5cm x 185.5cm). Layer the quilt top, batting and backing and baste together (see page 112). Using a toning thread, stitch-in-the-ditch along the seam lines of the 4 patch blocks as shown in red on the quilting diagram. By hand using the cotton à broder no. 16 threads, Quilt an echo pattern in the background of the pieced strips (pink on the SC 36, soft lilac on the SC 14) and vertical lines to separate and highlight the stripes in the vertical strips as shown in black in the quilting diagram. Trim the quilt edges and attach the binding (see page 113).

Quilting Diagram

Soft Boxes ★ ★

LIZA PRIOR LUCY

These colourful soft boxes have many practical uses, from bread on the supper table, to keeping your sewing bits and bobs tidy. If you use your box for holding edibles, we recommend making a washable liner to place inside the box.

SIZE OF BOXES
See the table opposite for details.

MATERIALS
Fabrics:
For each box you will need ¹/₂yd (45cm) each of two co-ordinating fabrics. Liza chose the following combinations:
Small Square Box **(A):**
Paperweight Pumpkin GP20-PN with Damask Plum Gold GP02-PG
Large Square Box **(B):**
Paperweight Sludge GP20-SL with

Damask Sage GP02-SA
Long Rectangle Box **(C):**
Paperweight Cobalt GP20-CB with Damask Smoky Blue GP02-SM

Batting:
See table opposite for quantities.

Other Materials:
Box weight cardboard or photographic mount board are suitable for this project. See table opposite for quantities.
PVA or other fabric glue.

CUTTING OUT: (See table opposite)

MAKING THE TIES
Take 1 strip 1in (2.5cm) x width of fabric, Place right side down and fold the raw edges to the centre of the strip as shown in diagram a, press. Fold the strip in half with the raw edges inside the fold, press and stitch as shown in diagram b. Cut the ties into 4 equal sections, each about 11in (28cm) long (a diagonal cut will prevent fraying). Repeat with the second strip to make a total of 8 ties.

MAKING THE BOX
Cut the card and batting to the sizes indicated in the chart above. Glue one piece of batting to each piece of card.

Take 1 piece of fabric and place right side up. On all sides measure (Boxes **A** and **C**) 2in (5cm), (Box **B**) 2.5in (6.5cm) from each corner and mark with a pencil. Carefully place one tie at each of the pencil marks and pin in place as shown in diagram c. Place your second piece of fabric right sides together with the first, enclosing the ties. Using a ¹/₄in (6mm) seam allowance, stitch around the edge of the fabric leaving a gap as shown in diagram d. Turn the fabric right side out and press.

With a ruler and pencil, lightly mark the fabric that will be on the inside of the box, with a fine line parallel to each side (Boxes **A** and **C**) 2in (5cm), (Box **B**) 2.5in (6.5cm) from the edge as shown in diagram e. Take 1 piece of card that matches the end farthest from the opening, place inside the fabric pocket batting side up between the vertical pencil lines. Stitch using a zipper foot along the horizontal pencil line immediately below the card as shown in diagram f. Next take the two side pieces of card, place in position batting side up and stitch in the same manner. Slip the large base card into the central section and stitch in place. Finally add the last piece of card and slip stitch the opening closed. Knot the ties to complete the box.

Box	Batting and Board	Fabric
Small Square Box (A) Finished Base Size 8in x 8in (20cm x 20cm)	Cut 4 pieces 2in x 8in (5cm x 20cm) Cut 1 piece 8in x 8in (20cm x 20cm)	Cut 2 pieces 13¾in x 13¾in (35cm x 35cm) Cut 2 strips 1in (2.5cm) x width of fabric
Large Square Box (B) Finished Base Size 10in x 10in (25.5cm x 25.5cm)	Cut 4 pieces 2½in x 10in (6.5cm x 25.5cm) Cut 1 piece 10in x 10in (25.5cm x 25.5cm)	Cut 2 pieces 16¾in x 16¾in (42.5cm x 42.5cm) Cut 2 strips 1in (2.5cm) x width of fabric
Long Rectangle Box (C) Finished Base Size 4in x 12in (10cm x 30.5cm)	Cut 2 pieces 2in x 4in (5cm x 10cm) Cut 2 pieces 2in x 12in (5cm x 30.5cm) Cut 1 piece 4in x 12in (10cm x 30.5cm)	Cut 2 pieces 9¾in x 17¾in (24.75cm x 45cm) Cut 2 strips 1in (2.5cm) x width of fabric

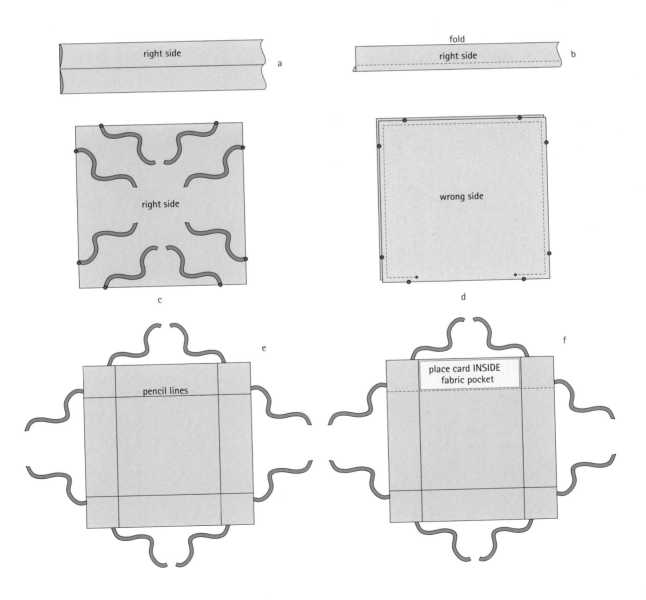

Soft Boxes - Liza Prior Lucy

Big Diamond Quilt ★

KAFFE FASSETT

An early 19th Century Dutch quilt caught my eye with its simple triangle block adding up to a bold diamond pattern. It was a good one for these new bronzy tones.

SIZE OF QUILT
The finished quilt will measure approx. 74in x 61in (188cm x 155cm).

MATERIALS
Patchwork Fabrics:
ROMAN GLASS
Jewel   GP01-J: 1/4yd (25cm)
DOTTY
Plum   GP14-P: 1/4yd (25cm)
PEONY
Maroon   GP17-MR: 1/4yd (25cm)
FRUIT BASKET
Black   GP19-BK: 1/4yd (25cm)
ALTERNATE STRIPE
               AS 01: 1/4yd (25cm)

BROAD CHECK
               BC 02: 1/4yd (25cm)
DOUBLE IKAT POLKA
Pumpkin   DiP 02: 1/4yd (25cm)
Denim   DiP 04: 1/4yd (25cm)
               or use leftovers from backing.
EXOTIC STRIPE
               ES 04: 1/2yd (45cm)
               ES 10: 1/4yd (25cm)
NARROW CHECK
               NC 02: 1/4yd (25cm)
               NC 05: 1/4yd (25cm)
NARROW STRIPE
               NS 13: 1/4yd (25cm)
PACHRANGI STRIPE
               PS 05: 1/4yd (25cm)

ROWAN STRIPE
               RS 04: 1/2yd (45cm)
SINGLE IKAT WASH
Banana   SiW 03: 1/2yd (45cm)
Red   SiW 06: 1/4yd (25cm)
SHOT COTTON
Slate   SC 04: 1/4yd (25cm)
Mustard   SC 16: 1/4yd (25cm)
Sage   SC 17: 1/4yd (25cm)
Pewter   SC 22: 1/4yd (25cm)
Mushroom   SC 31: 1/2yd (45cm)

Inner Border Fabric:
PEONY
Maroon   GP17-MR: 5/8yd (60cm)
Outer Border Fabric:
FRUIT BASKET
Black   GP19-BK: 1/2yd (45cm)
Backing Fabric:
DOUBLE IKAT POLKA
Denim   DiP 04: 3 3/4yds (3.5m)
Binding Fabric:
ROMAN GLASS
Jewel   GP01-J: 1/2yd (45cm)
Batting:
78in x 65in (198cm x 165cm).
Quilting threads:
Toning machine quilting thread.
Black hand quilting thread
Coats multicolour quilting thread, shade 885 Brookstones

Templates:
see page 108

PATCH SHAPES
A single triangle patch shape (Template Z) is used for this striking quilt. Inner and outer borders complete the quilt with a framing effect.

CUTTING OUT
Template Z: Cut 7 3/8in (18.75cm) wide strips. Each strip will give you 10 patches per 45in (114cm) wide fabric.
Cut 15 in ES04, 13 in SiW 03, 12 in RS 04, 11 in SC 31, 8 in GP17-MR, GP19-BK, AS 01, ES 10, SC 22, 7 in GP01-J, DiP 02, NC 02, SC 17, 6 in DiP 04, SiW 06, 5 in PS 05, SC 16, 4 in GP14-P, BC 02, NC 05, SC 04 and 3 in NS 13.
Inner Borders: Cut 6 strips 3 1/2in (9cm) wide x width of fabric in GP17-MR.

Quilt Assembly

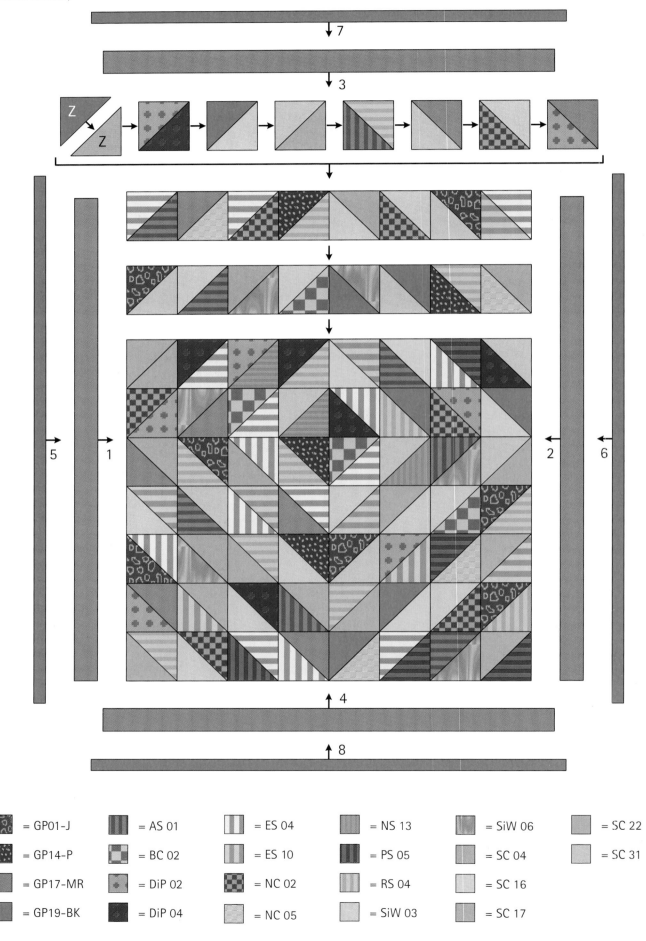

	= GP01-J		= AS 01		= ES 04		= NS 13		= SiW 06		= SC 22
	= GP14-P		= BC 02		= ES 10		= PS 05		= SC 04		= SC 31
	= GP17-MR		= DiP 02		= NC 02		= RS 04		= SC 16		
	= GP19-BK		= DiP 04		= NC 05		= SiW 03		= SC 17		

Outer Borders: Cut 7 strips 2in (5cm) wide x width of fabric in GP19-BK.

Binding: Cut 7 strips 2¹/₂in (6.25cm) wide x width of fabric in GP01-J.

Backing: Cut 1 piece 65in x 45in (165cm by 114cm) and 1 piece 65in x 34in (165cm by 86cm) in DiP 04.

MAKING THE QUILT
Using a ¹/₄in (6mm) seam allowance throughout. Referring to the quilt assembly diagram for fabric combinations, piece 80 square blocks. Join the blocks into 10 rows of 8 blocks, Join the rows to form the quilt centre.

ADDING THE BORDERS
Join the inner border strips as necessary and cut 2 inner borders each 65¹/₂in x 3¹/₂in (166.5cm x 9cm) for the quilt sides and 2 inner borders each 58¹/₂in x 3¹/₂in (148.5cm x 9cm) for the quilt top and bottom. Add the inner borders to the quilt centre in the order indicated by the quilt assembly diagram. Join the outer border strips as necessary and cut 2 outer borders each 71¹/₂in x 2in (181.5cm x 5cm) for the quilt sides and 2 outer borders each 61¹/₂in x 2in (156.25cm x 5cm) for the quilt top and bottom. Add the outer borders to the quilt centre in the order indicated by the quilt assembly diagram.

FINISHING THE QUILT
Press the quilt top. Seam the backing pieces using a ¹/₄in (6mm) seam allowance to form a piece approx. 78in x 65in (198cm x 165cm). Layer the quilt top, batting and backing and baste together (see page 112). This quilt is machine quilted in the ditch to emphasize the diamond design and stabilize the quilt using a toning machine quilting thread, then hand quilted in rows for a softer effect, as shown in the quilting diagram. The 'darker' sections are quilted with a black hand quilting thread and the 'pale' sections are quilted using Coats multicolour quilting thread shade 885. The diagram shows the quilt centre, continue in the same manner to the quilt edge. Trim the quilt edges and attach the binding (see page 113).

Quilting Diagram

Blue Stars Quilt ★★

KAFFE FASSETT

*This layout always intrigues me. I emphasized the star like elements.
The cool blues and white is nicely set off by the sage green.*

SIZE OF QUILT
The finished quilt will measure approx.
74in x 63in (188cm x 160cm).

MATERIALS
Patchwork Fabrics:
Note: The fabric quantities are closely
specified, allowing for very little waste, so
cut carefully (or buy a little more!)
ROMAN GLASS
Blue and White   GP01-BW: ¹/₄yd (25cm)
DAMASK
Smoky Blue   GP02-SM: ¹/₄yd (25cm)
FLORAL DANCE
Blue   GP12-B: ¹/₄yd (25cm)
CHRYSANTHEMUM
Blue   GP13-B: ¹/₄yd (25cm)

DOTTY
Lavender   GP14-L: ¹/₄yd (25cm)
Sea Green   GP14-SG: ¹/₈yd (15cm)
BUBBLES
Cobalt   GP15-C: ¹/₄yd (25cm)
Plum   GP15-P: ¹/₄yd (25cm)
Sky Blue   GP15-S: ⁷/₈yd (80cm)
MOSAIC
Purple   GP16-PU: ³/₈yd (35cm)
PEONY
Blue   GP17-BL: ³/₈yd (35cm)
Grey   GP17-GR: ¹/₈yd (15cm)
Violet   GP17-VI: ¹/₈yd (15cm)
FRUIT BASKET
Taupe   GP19-TA: ¹/₄yd (25cm)
DOUBLE IKAT CHECKERBOARD
Magenta   DiC 02: ¹/₄yd (25cm)

DOUBLE IKAT POLKA
Sage   DiP 01: ¹/₄yd (25cm)
Blue   DiP 05: ¹/₄yd (25cm)
EXOTIC STRIPE
   ES 15: ¹/₄yd (25cm)
OMBRE STRIPE
   OS 02: ¹/₈yd (15cm)
   OS 05: ¹/₈yd (15cm)
ROWAN STRIPE
   RS 02: ¹/₄yd (25cm)
   RS 05: ¹/₄yd (25cm)
   RS 06: ¹/₈yd (15cm)

SHOT COTTON
Opal   SC 05: ¹/₄yd (25cm)
Lavender   SC 14: ¹/₈yd (15cm)
Duck Egg   SC 26: ¹/₄yd (25cm)
Border Fabric:
CHRYSANTHEMUM
Blue   GP13-B: 1yd (90cm)
Backing Fabric:
DOUBLE IKAT POLKA
Sage   DiP 01: 4yds (3.6m)
Binding Fabric:
BUBBLES
Sky Blue   GP15-S:
   see patchwork fabrics
Batting:
78in x 67in (198cm x 170cm).
Quilting thread:
Toning hand or machine quilting thread.

Templates:
see page 102

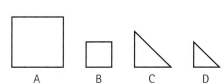

A   B   C   D

PATCH SHAPES
Two square patch shapes (Template A and
B) and two triangle patch shapes
(Template C and D) are pieced to make
traditional sawtooth star blocks for this
quilt.

CUTTING OUT
Note: Cut the patch shapes in the order
specified, always keeping remaining
fabric in the largest size possible. Don't
worry about the stripe direction too
much, this quilt is supposed to be
'scrap style'.

Template A: Cut 6in (15.25cm) wide strips. Cut 3 in GP02-SM, GP12-B, GP13-B, GP15-SB, GP16-PU, DiC 02, 2 in GP17-BL, DiP 01, DiP 05, ES 15, 1 in GP14-L, GP15-C, GP15-P and RS 02.
Template B: Cut 3¼in (8.25cm) wide strips. Cut 20 in GP01-BW, GP17-BL, 16 in GP19-TA, 12 in GP17-VI, RS 05, 8 in RS 02, 4 in GP14-L, GP14-SG, GP15-C, GP15-P, GP16-PU, GP17-GR, OS 02 and RS 06.
Template C: Cut 3⅜in (8.5cm) wide strips. Cut 20 in SC26, 16 in SC 05, 12 in RS 05, SC 14, 8 in GP14-SG, ES 15, OS 02, RS 02, RS 06, 4 in GP14-L, GP15-S, GP19-TA, DiP 01 and OS 05.
Template D: Cut 3⅝in (9.25cm) wide strips. Cut 24 in GP02-SM, GP12-B, GP15-S, GP16-PU, DiC 02, 16 in GP13-B, GP15-C, GP17-B, DiP 01, DiP 05, ES 15, 8 in GP14-L, GP15-P and RS 02.

Borders: Cut 7 strips 4½in (11.5cm) wide x width of fabric in GP13-B.

Binding: Cut 7 strips 2½in (6.25cm) wide x width of fabric in GP15-S.

Backing: Cut 1 piece 67in x 45in (170cm by 114cm) and 1 piece 67in x 33in (170cm by 84cm) in DiP 01.

MAKING THE QUILT

Using a ¼in (6mm) seam allowance throughout, piece 30 blocks as shown in block assembly diagrams a and b, referring to the quilt assembly diagram for fabric placement.
Join the blocks into 6 rows of 5 blocks, Join the rows to form the quilt centre.

ADDING THE BORDERS

Join the border strips as necessary and cut 2 borders each 55½in x 4½in (141cm x 11.5cm) for the quilt top and bottom and 2 borders each 74½in x 4½in (189.25cm x 11.5cm) for the quilt sides. Add the borders to the quilt centre in the order indicated by the quilt assembly diagram.

FINISHING THE QUILT

Press the quilt top.
Seam the backing pieces using a ¼in (6mm) seam allowance to form a piece approx. 78in x 67in (198cm x 170cm). Layer the quilt top, batting and backing and baste together (see page 112). Using a toning thread, stitch-in-the-ditch along the seam lines, between the patches by hand or machine. Trim the quilt edges and attach the binding (see page 113).

Block Assembly

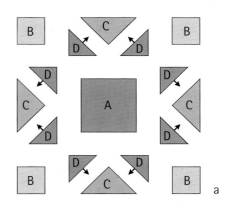

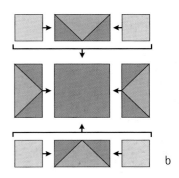

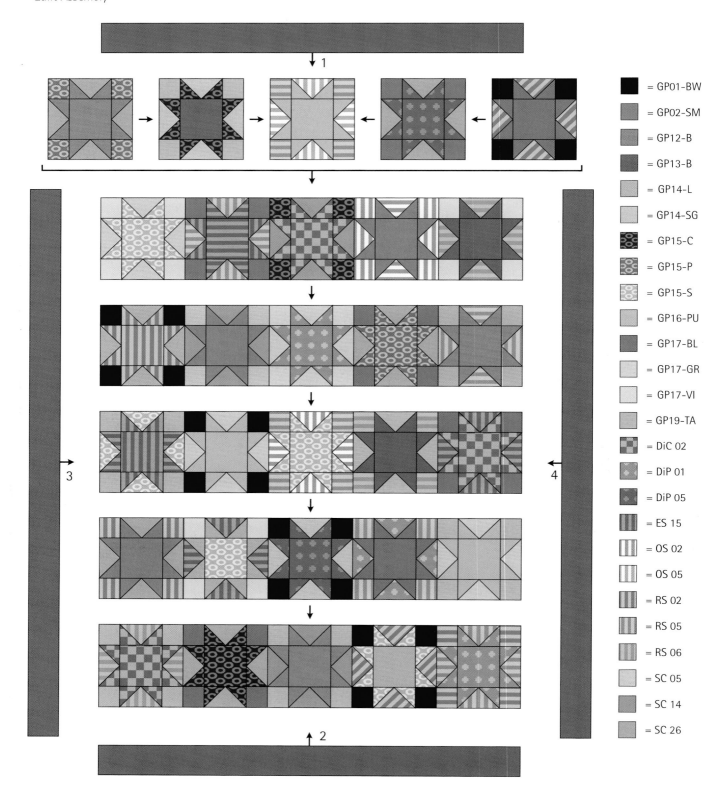

= GP01–BW
= GP02–SM
= GP12–B
= GP13–B
= GP14–L
= GP14–SG
= GP15–C
= GP15–P
= GP15–S
= GP16–PU
= GP17–BL
= GP17–GR
= GP17–VI
= GP19–TA
= DiC 02
= DiP 01
= DiP 05
= ES 15
= OS 02
= OS 05
= RS 02
= RS 05
= RS 06
= SC 05
= SC 14
= SC 26

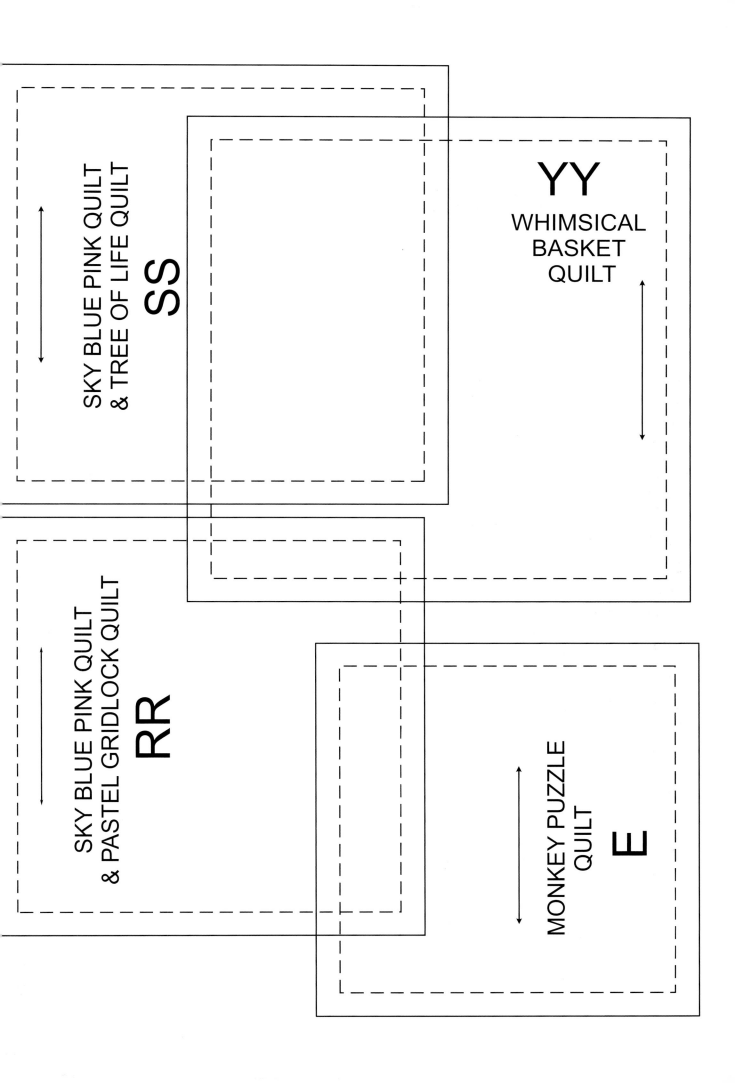

SS

SKY BLUE PINK QUILT
& TREE OF LIFE QUILT

YY

WHIMSICAL
BASKET
QUILT

RR

SKY BLUE PINK QUILT
& PASTEL GRIDLOCK QUILT

E

MONKEY PUZZLE
QUILT

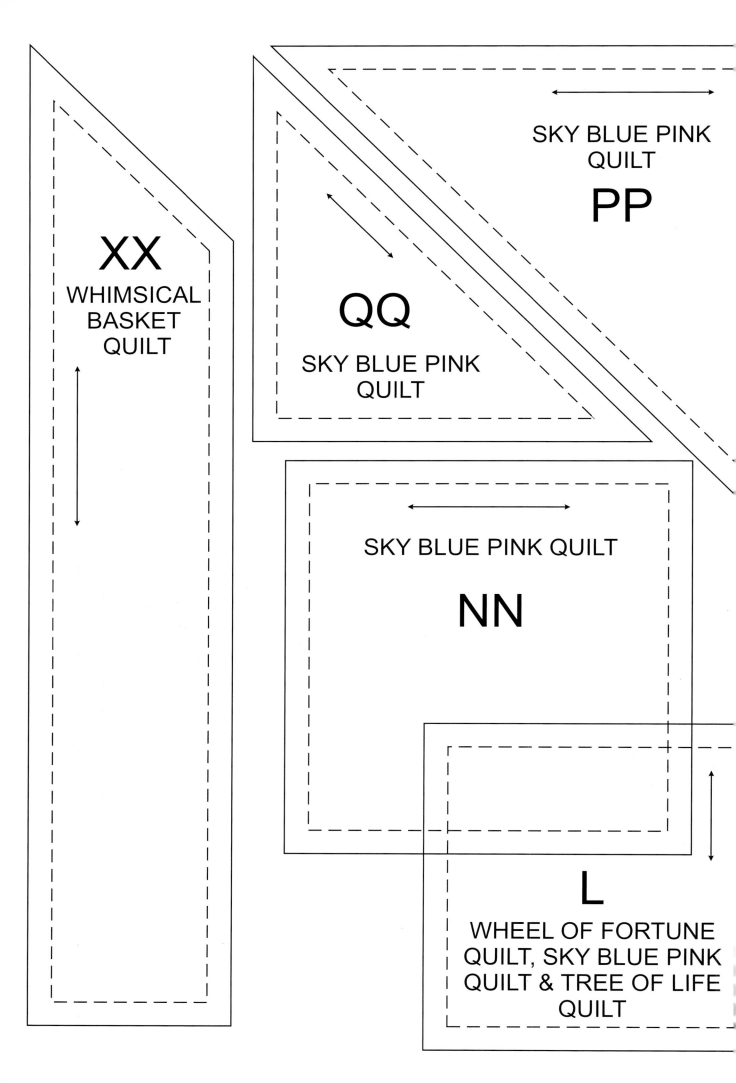

XX
WHIMSICAL
BASKET
QUILT

QQ
SKY BLUE PINK
QUILT

SKY BLUE PINK
QUILT
PP

SKY BLUE PINK QUILT
NN

L
WHEEL OF FORTUNE
QUILT, SKY BLUE PINK
QUILT & TREE OF LIFE
QUILT

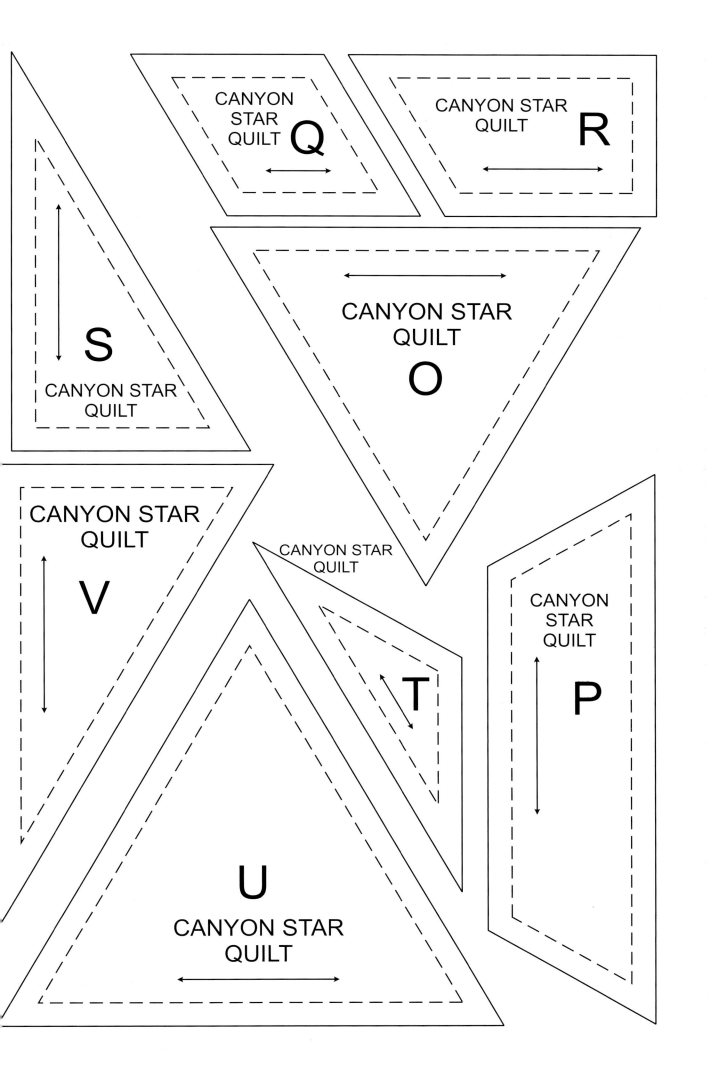

CANYON STAR QUILT Q

CANYON STAR QUILT R

CANYON STAR QUILT O

S CANYON STAR QUILT

CANYON STAR QUILT V

CANYON STAR QUILT T

CANYON STAR QUILT P

U CANYON STAR QUILT

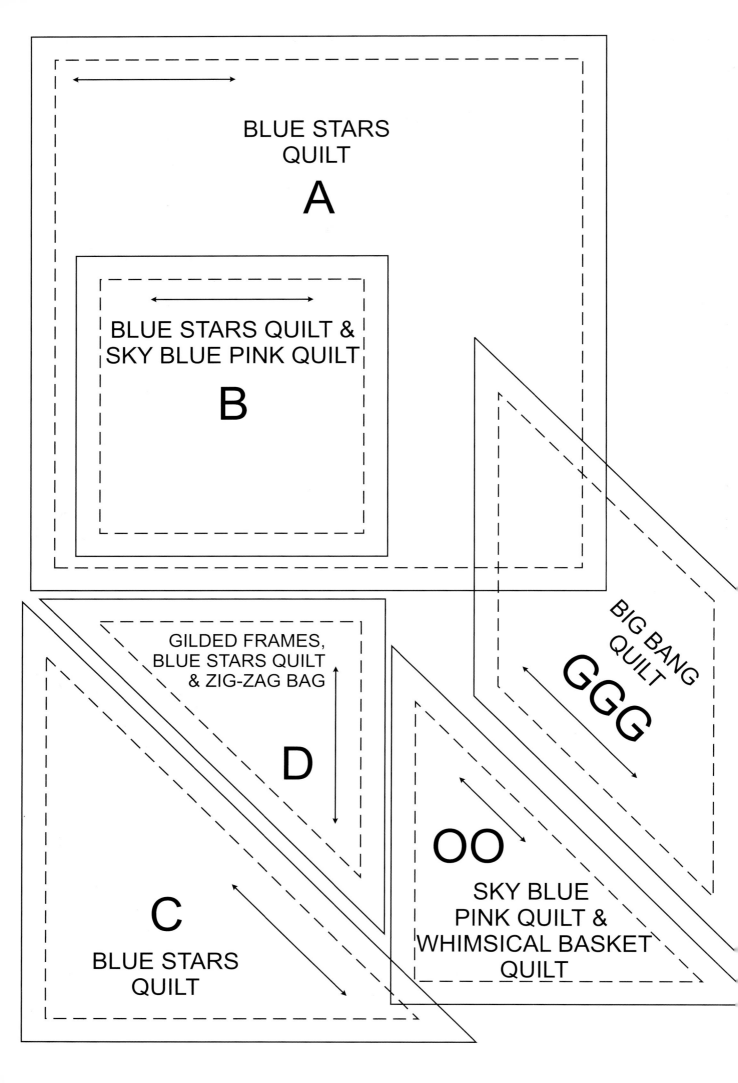

BLUE STARS
QUILT

A

BLUE STARS QUILT &
SKY BLUE PINK QUILT

B

GILDED FRAMES,
BLUE STARS QUILT
& ZIG-ZAG BAG

D

C

BLUE STARS
QUILT

OO

SKY BLUE
PINK QUILT &
WHIMSICAL BASKET
QUILT

BIG BANG
QUILT

GGG

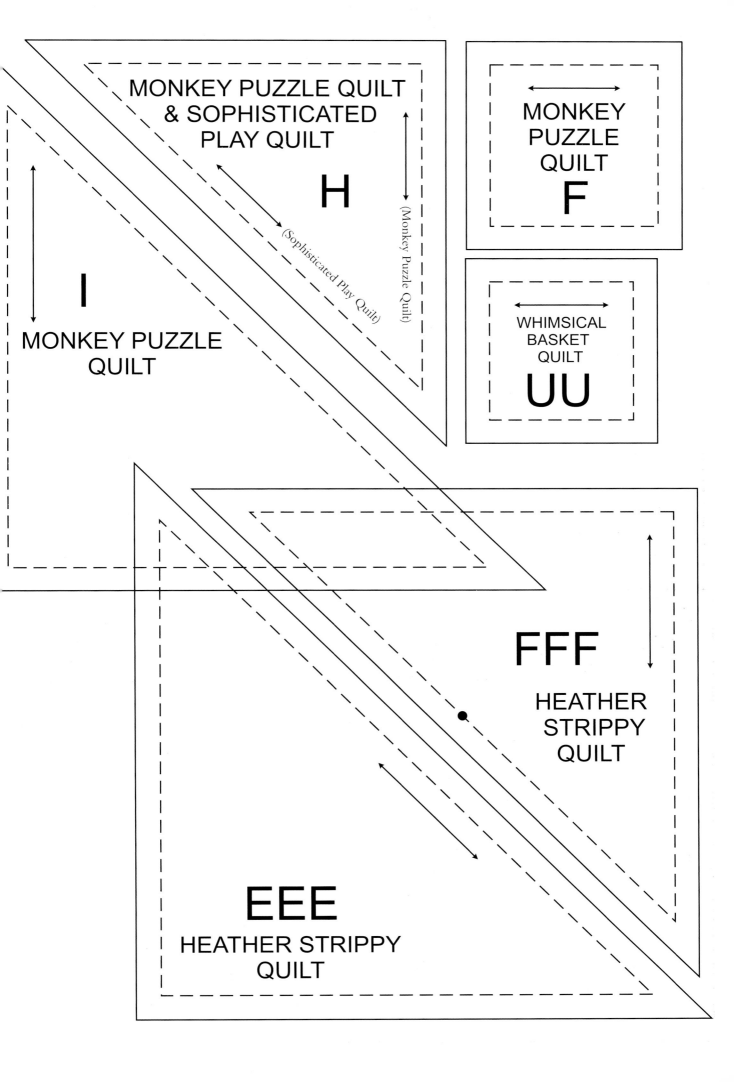

MONKEY PUZZLE QUILT
& SOPHISTICATED
PLAY QUILT

H

(Sophisticated Play Quilt)

(Monkey Puzzle Quilt)

I

MONKEY PUZZLE
QUILT

MONKEY
PUZZLE
QUILT

F

WHIMSICAL
BASKET
QUILT

UU

FFF

HEATHER
STRIPPY
QUILT

EEE

HEATHER STRIPPY
QUILT

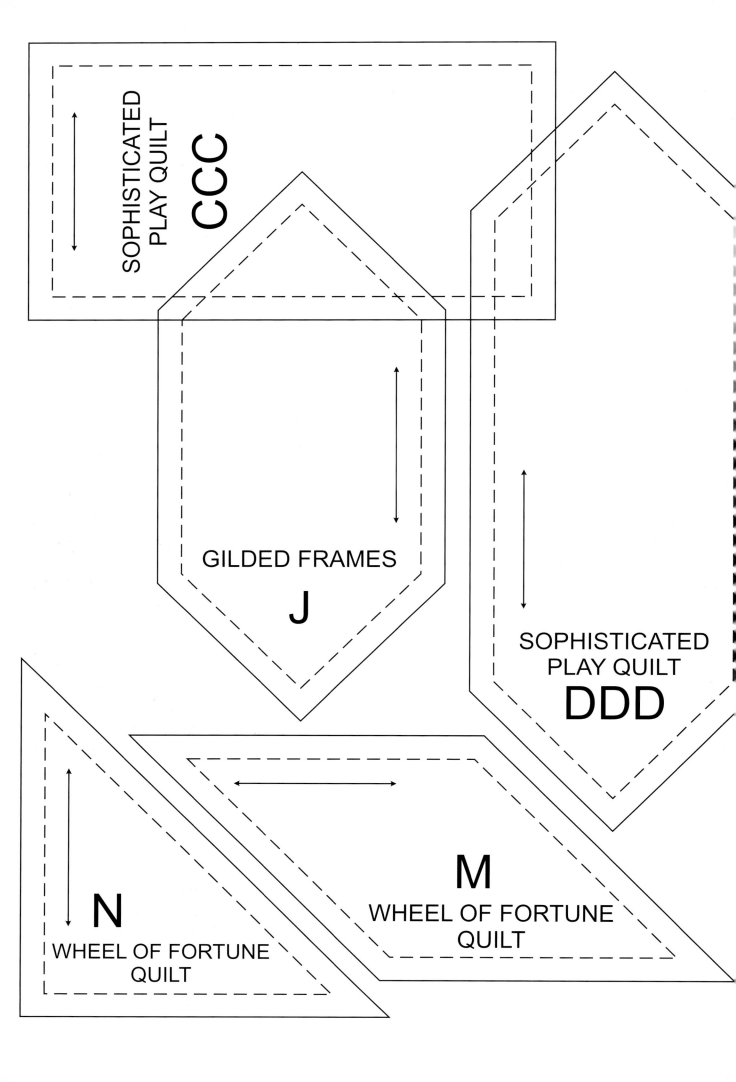

SOPHISTICATED
PLAY QUILT
CCC

GILDED FRAMES
J

SOPHISTICATED
PLAY QUILT
DDD

N
WHEEL OF FORTUNE
QUILT

M
WHEEL OF FORTUNE
QUILT

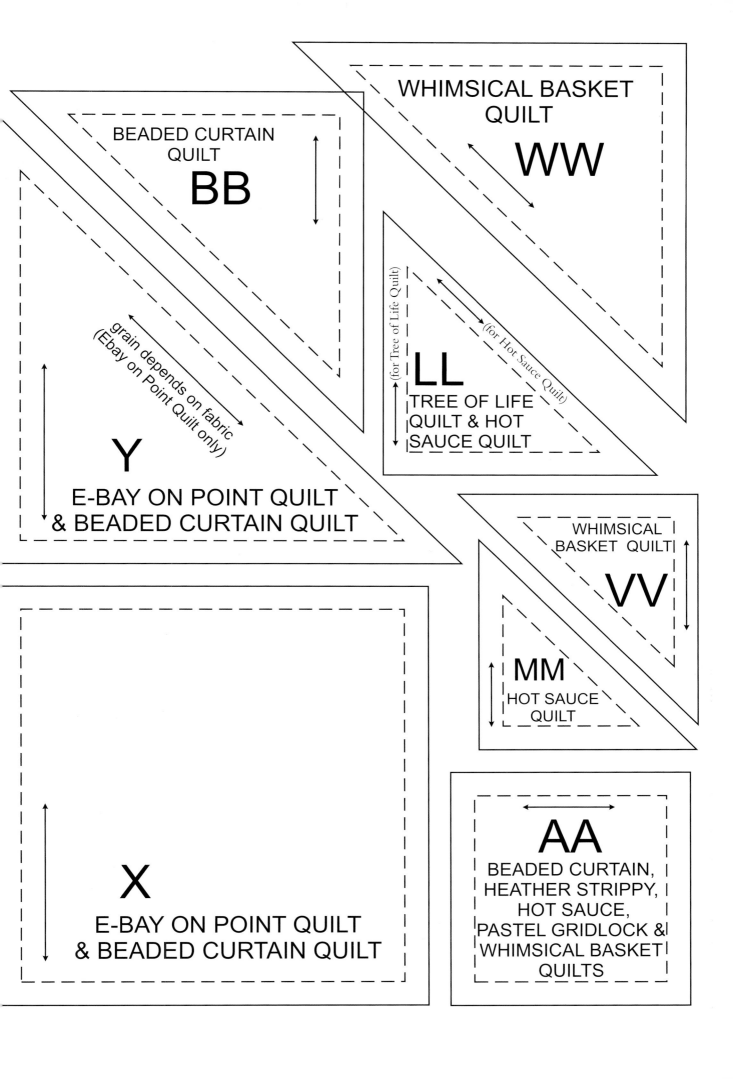

BEADED CURTAIN
QUILT

BB

WHIMSICAL BASKET
QUILT

WW

grain depends on fabric
(Ebay on Point Quilt only)

Y

E-BAY ON POINT QUILT
& BEADED CURTAIN QUILT

(for Tree of Life Quilt)

(for Hot Sauce Quilt)

LL

TREE OF LIFE
QUILT & HOT
SAUCE QUILT

WHIMSICAL
BASKET QUILT

VV

MM

HOT SAUCE
QUILT

X

E-BAY ON POINT QUILT
& BEADED CURTAIN QUILT

AA

BEADED CURTAIN,
HEATHER STRIPPY,
HOT SAUCE,
PASTEL GRIDLOCK &
WHIMSICAL BASKET
QUILTS

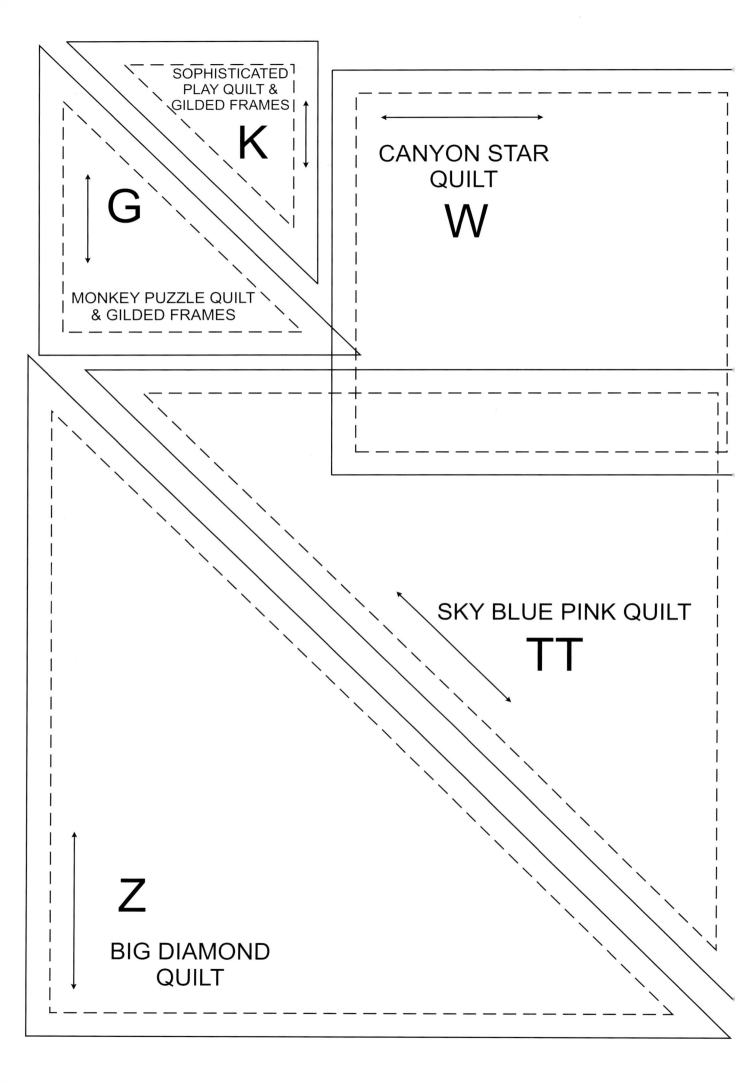

SOPHISTICATED
PLAY QUILT &
GILDED FRAMES

K

G

MONKEY PUZZLE QUILT
& GILDED FRAMES

CANYON STAR
QUILT

W

SKY BLUE PINK QUILT

TT

Z

BIG DIAMOND
QUILT

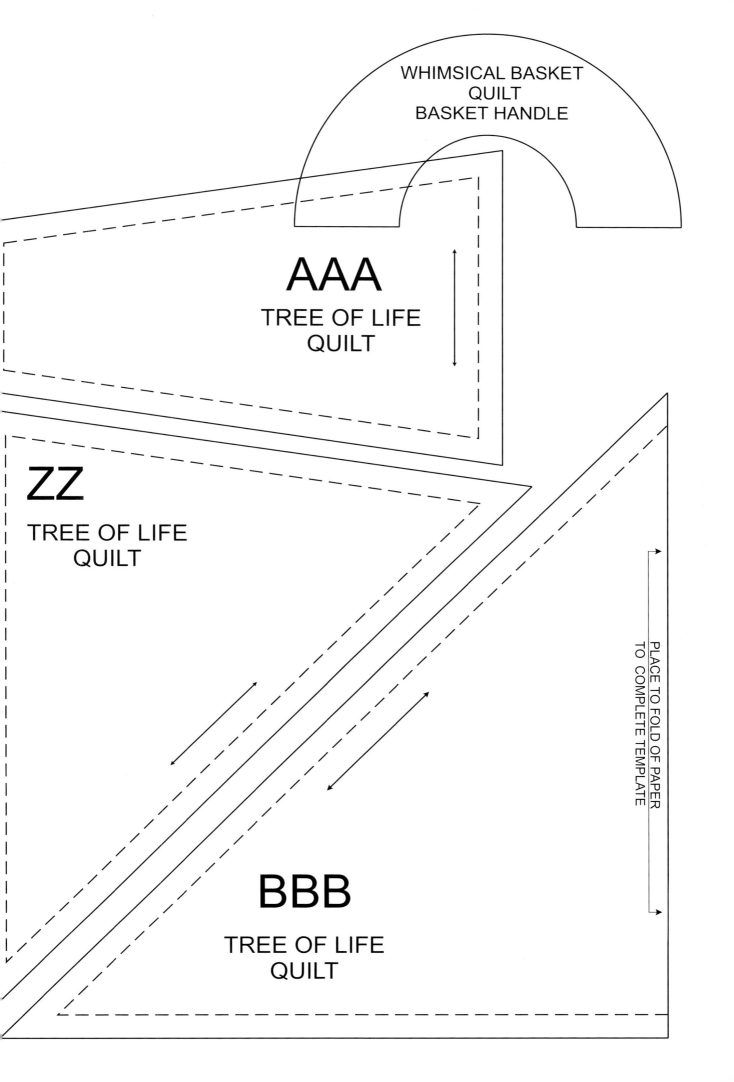

WHIMSICAL BASKET
QUILT
BASKET HANDLE

AAA
TREE OF LIFE
QUILT

ZZ

TREE OF LIFE
QUILT

PLACE TO FOLD OF PAPER
TO COMPLETE TEMPLATE

BBB

TREE OF LIFE
QUILT

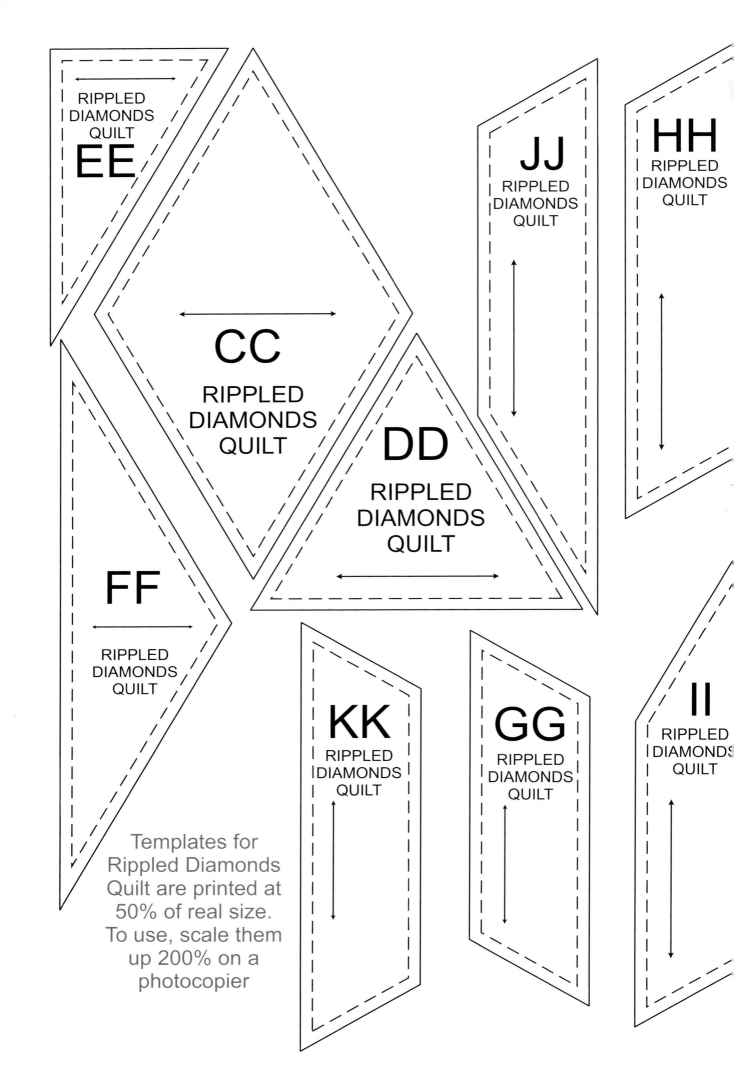

RIPPLED DIAMONDS QUILT

EE

CC
RIPPLED DIAMONDS QUILT

DD
RIPPLED DIAMONDS QUILT

FF
RIPPLED DIAMONDS QUILT

JJ
RIPPLED DIAMONDS QUILT

HH
RIPPLED DIAMONDS QUILT

KK
RIPPLED DIAMONDS QUILT

GG
RIPPLED DIAMONDS QUILT

II
RIPPLED DIAMONDS QUILT

Templates for Rippled Diamonds Quilt are printed at 50% of real size. To use, scale them up 200% on a photocopier

Patchwork Know How

These instructions are intended for the novice quilt maker, providing the basic information needed to make the projects in this book, along with some useful tips.

Preparing the fabric

Prewash all new fabrics before you begin, to ensure that there will be no uneven shrinkage and no bleeding of colours when the quilt is laundered. Press the fabric whilst it is still damp to return crispness to it.

Making templates

Transparent template plastic is the best material, it is durable and allows you to see the fabric and select certain motifs. You can also use thin stiff cardboard.

Templates for machine-piecing

1 Trace off the actual-sized template provided either directly on to template plastic, or tracing paper, and then on to thin cardboard. Use a ruler to help you trace off the straight cutting line, dotted seam line and grainlines. Some of the templates in this book are so large that we have only been able to give you half of them. Before transferring them on to plastic or card, trace off the half template, place the fold edge up to the fold of a piece of paper, and carefully draw around the shape. Cut out the paper double thickness, and open out for the completed template.

2 Cut out the traced off template using a craft knife, ruler and a self-healing cutting mat.

3 Punch holes in the corners of the template, at each point on the seam line, using a hole punch.

Templates for hand-piecing

• Make a template as for machine piecing, but do not trace off the cutting line. Use the dotted seam line as the outer edge of the template.

• This template allows you to draw the seam lines directly on to the fabric. The seam allowances can then be cut by eye around the patch.

Cutting the fabric

On the individual instructions for each patchwork, you will find a summary of all the patch shapes used.
Always mark and cut out any border and binding strips first, followed by the largest patch shapes and finally the smallest ones, to make the most efficient use of your fabric. The border and binding strips are best cut using a rotary cutter.

Rotary cutting

Rotary cut strips are usually cut across the fabric from selvedge to selvedge.

1 Before beginning to cut, press out any folds or creases in the fabric. If you are cutting a large piece of fabric, you will need to fold it several times to fit the cutting mat. When there is only a single fold, place the fold facing you. If the fabric is too wide to be folded only once, fold it concertina-style until it fits your mat. A small rotary cutter with a sharp blade will cut up to 6 layers of fabric; a large cutter up to 8 layers.

2 To ensure that your cut strips are straight and even, the folds must be placed exactly parallel to the straight edges of the fabric and along a line on the cutting mat.

3 Place a plastic ruler over the raw edge of the fabric, overlapping it about 1/2in (1.25cm). Make sure that the ruler is at right angles to both the straight edges and the fold to ensure that you cut along the straight grain. Press down on the ruler and wheel the cutter away from yourself along the edge of the ruler.

4 Open out the fabric to check the edge. Don't worry if it's not perfectly straight; a little wiggle will not show when the quilt is stitched together. Re-fold fabric, then place the ruler over the trimmed edge, aligning edge with the markings on the ruler that match the correct strip width. Cut strip along the edge of the ruler.

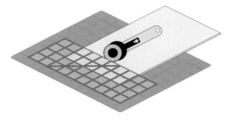

Using templates

The most efficient way to cut out templates is by first rotary cutting a strip of fabric the width stated for your template, and then marking off your templates along the strip, edge to edge at the required angle. This method leaves hardly any waste and gives a random effect to your patches.
A less efficient method is to fussy cut, where the templates are cut individually by placing them on particular motifs or stripes, to create special effects. Although this method is more wasteful it yields very interesting results.

1 Place the template face down on the wrong side of the fabric, with the grain line arrow following the straight grain of the fabric, if indicated. Be careful though - check with your individual instructions, as some instructions may ask you to cut patches on varying grains.

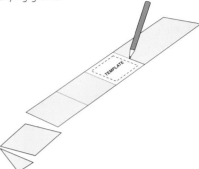

2 Hold the template firmly in place and draw around it with a sharp pencil or crayon, marking in the corner dots or seam lines. To save fabric, position patches close together or even touching. Don't worry if outlines positioned on the straight grain when drawn on striped fabrics do not always match the stripes when cut - this will add a degree of visual excitement to the patchwork!

3 Once you've drawn all the pieces needed, you are ready to cut the fabric, with either a rotary cutter and ruler, or a pair of sharp sewing scissors.

Basic hand- and machine-piecing

Patches can be joined together by hand or machine. Machine stitching is quicker, but hand assembly allows you to carry your patches around with you and work on them in every spare moment. The choice is yours. For techniques that are new to you, practise on scrap pieces of fabric until you feel confident.

Machine-piecing

Follow the quilt instructions for the order in which to piece the individual patchwork blocks and then assemble the blocks together in rows.

1 Seam lines are not marked on the fabric, so stitch 1/4in (6mm) seams using the machine needle plate, a 1/4in- (6mm-) wide machine foot, or tape stuck to the machine as a guide. Pin two patches with right sides together, matching edges.

Set your machine at 10-12 stitches per inch (2.5cm) and stitch seams from edge to edge, removing pins as you feed the fabric through the machine.

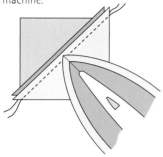

2 Press the seams of each patchwork block to one side before attempting to join it to another block.

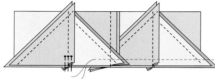

3 When joining rows of blocks, make sure that adjacent seam allowances are pressed in opposite directions to reduce bulk and make matching easier. Pin pieces together directly through the stitch line and to the right and left of the seam. Remove pins as you sew. Continue pressing seams to one side as you work.

Hand-piecing

1 Pin two patches with right sides together, so that the marked seam lines are facing outwards.

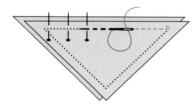

2 Using a single strand of strong thread, secure the corner of a seam line with a couple of back stitches.

3 Sew running stitches along the marked line, working 8-10 stitches per inch (2.5cm) and ending at the opposite seam line corner with a few back stitches. When hand piecing never stitch over the seam allowances.

4 Press the seams to one side, as shown in machine piecing (Step 2).

English Hand-piecing over Papers

This traditional style of hand piecing produces beautifully accurate results and has the added bonus of being very portable, prepare a few patches in advance and take them anywhere to enjoy a quiet relaxing moment.

1 Using the patchwork templates for your chosen project, make two master templates from template plastic or stiff card. The first template is used for cutting your fabric the correct size and is traced using the outer solid line. The second template is traced from the inner broken line. This is used to mark and cut paper templates. Cut enough paper templates to complete your project, standard 80gsm paper is ideal for this purpose. Cut the fabric according to the project instructions.

2 Pin the paper template to the wrong side of the fabric patch making sure the paper is in the centre of the fabric. Starting on one side of the patch fold the fabric over the paper template and tack into place through the paper, work around the patch folding in the corners carefully as you go. Prepare enough patches to complete a block in this way.

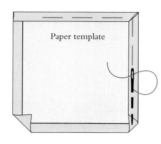

3 Referring to the project instructions for the correct sequence, take the first two fabric patches, place right sides together and whip stitch along the matching edge, open out, take the next patch and add in the same manner. Do not remove papers until a patch shape is completely enclosed by other patches on all sides.

Inset seams.

In some patchwork layouts a patch will have to be sewn into an angled corner formed by the joining of two other patches. Use the following method whether you are machine or hand-piecing. Don't be intimidated - this is not hard to do once you have learned a couple of techniques. The seam is sewn from the centre outwards in two halves to ensure that no tucks appear at the centre.

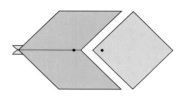

1 Mark with dots exactly where the inset will be joined and mark the seam lines on the wrong side of the fabric on the inset patch.

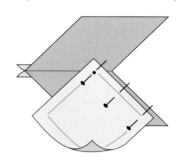

2 With right sides together and inset piece on top, pin through the dots to match the inset points. Pin the rest of the seam at right angles to the stitching line, along one edge of an adjoining patch.

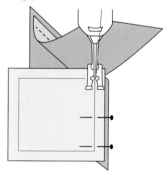

3 Stitch the patch in place along the seam line starting with the needle down through the inset point dots. Secure thread with a backstitch if hand-piecing, or stitch forward for a few stitches before backstitching, when machine-piecing.

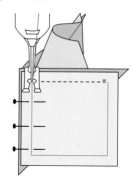

4 Pivot the patch, to enable it to align with the adjacent side of the angled corner, allowing you work on the second half of the seam. Starting with a pin at the inset point once again. Pin and stitch the second side in place, as before. Check seams and press carefully.

Machine appliqué
Using adhesive web:

To make machine appliqué even easier you can use adhesive web, which comes attached to a paper backing sheet, to bond the motifs to the background fabric. This keeps the pieces in place whilst they are being stitched.

1 Trace the appliqué design onto tracing paper. Reverse the tracing paper to reverse the image. Place the adhesive web (paper side up) over the reversed image and trace the motifs leaving a 1/4in (6mm) gap between all the shapes. Roughly cut out the motifs 1/8in (3mm) outside your drawn line.

2 Bond the motifs to the reverse of your chosen fabrics. Cut out on the drawn line with very sharp scissors. Remove the backing paper by scoring in the centre of the motif carefully with a scissor point and peeling the paper away from the centre out, this prevents damage to the edges. Place the motifs onto the background noting any which may be layered. Cover with a clean cloth and bond with a hot iron (check instructions for temperature setting as adhesive web can vary depending on the manufacturer).

3 Using a contrasting or complimenting coloured thread in your machine, work small close zigzag stitches around the edge of the motifs making sure all the raw edges are stitched. Other decorative stitches can be used such as blanket stitch if you machine has them or you can stitch by hand.

Hand appliqué

Good preparation is essential for speedy and accurate hand appliqué. The finger-pressing method is suitable for needle-turning application, used for simple shapes like leaves and flowers. Using a card template is the best method for bold simple motifs such as circles.
Finger-pressing:

1 To make your template, transfer the appliqué design on to stiff card using carbon paper, and cut out template. Trace around the outline of your appliquéd shape on to the right side of your fabric using a well sharpened pencil. Cut out shapes, adding a 1/4 in (6mm) seam allowance all around by eye.

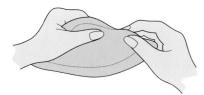

2 Hold shape right side up and fold under the seam, turning along your drawn line, pinch to form a crease. Dampening the fabric makes this very easy. When using shapes with 'points' such as leaves turn the seam

allowance at the 'point' in first as shown in the diagram, then continue all round the shape. If your shapes have sharp curves you can snip the seam allowance to ease the curve. Take care not to stretch the appliqué shapes as you work.

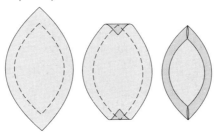

Card templates:

1 Cut out appliqué shapes as shown in step 1 of finger-pressing. Make a circular template from thin cardboard, without seam allowances.

2 Using a matching thread, work a row of running stitches close to the edge of the fabric circle. Place thin cardboard template in the centre of the fabric circle on the wrong side of the fabric.

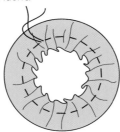

3 Carefully pull up the running stitches to gather up the edge of the fabric circle around the cardboard template. Press, so that no puckers or tucks appear on the right side. Then, carefully pop out the cardboard template without distorting the fabric shape.

Pressing stems:

For straight stems, place fabric strip face down and simply press over the 1/4 in (6mm) seam turning along each edge.

Bias Vines and Stems:

1 Bias cut strips of fabric twice the desired finished width of the vine plus _in (12mm). Fold the strip right side out matching the raw edges carefully and gently press. Lay the strip along the desired path and ease curves. Stitch the vine in place 1/4 in (6mm)

from the raw edge as shown in the diagram, this can be done by hand or machine.

2 Fold the free edge of the vine over to cover the raw edges, again easing the curves, and slipstitch in place using a thread matching the vine.

Needle-turning application:

1 Take the appliqué shape and pin in position. Stroke the seam allowance under with the tip of the needle as far as the creased pencil line, and hold securely in place with your thumb. Using a matching thread, bring the needle up from the back of the block into the edge of the shape and proceed to blind-hem in place. This is a stitch where the motifs appear to be held on invisibly. Bring the thread out from below through the folded edge of the motif, never on the top. The stitches must be worked small, even and close together to prevent the seam allowance from unfolding and frayed edges appearing. Try to avoid pulling the stitches too tight, as this will cause the motifs to pucker up. Work around the whole shape, stroking under each small section before sewing.

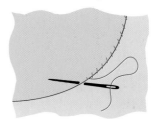

Mitreing Borders.

1 Centre the borders along the sides of the quilt and then stitch each into place stopping 1/4 in (6mm) from the end of the quilt centre.

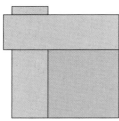

right side

2 Working on each corner in turn, fold the quilt at a 45 degree angle and stitch from the intersection of the two border seams to the outer edge of the borders as shown in the diagram. The stitching line should in effect extend the folded edge of the quilt.

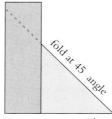

fold at 45 angle

wrong side

3 Open out the quilt and check the borders lay flat and the angle is correct. Finally, trim the excess border fabric back to 1/4 in (6mm).

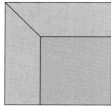

right side

Quilting and finishing

When you have finished piecing your patchwork and added any borders, press it carefully. It is now ready for quilting.

Marking quilting designs and motifs

Many tools are available for marking quilting patterns, check the manufacturer's instructions for use and test on scraps of fabric from your project. Use an acrylic ruler for marking straight lines.

Stencils: Some designs require stencils, these can be made at home, by transferring the designs on to template plastic, or stiff cardboard. The design is then cut away in the form of long dashes, to act as guides for both internal and external lines. These stencils are a quick method for producing an identical set of repeated designs.

Preparing the backing and batting

• Remove the selvedges and piece together the backing fabric to form a backing at least 3in (7.5cm) larger all round than the patchwork top.

• For quilting choose a fairly thin batting, preferably pure cotton, to give your quilt a flat appearance. If your batting has been rolled up, unroll it and let it rest before cutting it to the same size as the backing.

• For a large quilt it may be necessary to join 2 pieces of batting to fit. Lay the pieces of batting on a flat surface so that they overlap by approx 8in (20cm). Cut a curved line through both layers.

overlap wadding

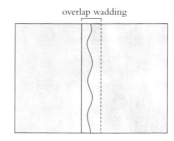

2 . Carefully peel away the two narrow pieces and discard. Butt the curved cut edges back together. Stitch the two pieces together using a large herringbone stitch.

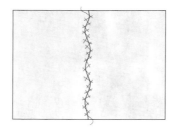

Basting the layers together

1 On a bare floor or large work surface, lay out the backing with wrong side uppermost. Use weights along the edges to keep it taut.

2 Lay the batting on the backing and smooth it out gently. Next lay the patchwork top, right side up, on top of the batting and smooth gently until there are no wrinkles. Pin at the corners and at the midpoints of each side, close to the edges.

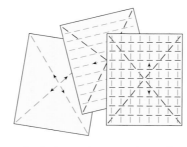

3 Beginning at the centre, baste diagonal lines outwards to the corners, making your stitches about 3in (7.5cm) long. Then, again starting at the centre, baste horizontal and vertical lines out to the edges. Continue basting until you have basted a grid of lines about 4in (10cm) apart over the entire quilt.

4 For speed, when machine quilting, some quilters prefer to baste their quilt sandwich layers together using rust-proof safety pins, spaced at 4in (10cm) intervals over the entire quilt.

Hand quilting

This is best done with the quilt mounted on a quilting frame or hoop, but as long as you have basted the quilt well, a frame is not essential. With the quilt top facing upwards, begin at the centre of the quilt and make even running stitches following the design. It is more important to make even stitches on both sides of the quilt than to make small ones. Start and finish your stitching with back stitches and bury the ends of your threads in the batting.

Machine quilting

• For a flat looking quilt, always use a walking foot on your machine for straight lines, and a darning foot for free-motion quilting.

• It's best to start your quilting at the centre of the quilt and work out towards the borders, doing the straight quilting lines first (stitch-in-the-ditch) followed by the free-motion quilting.

• When free motion quilting stitch in a loose meandering style as shown in the diagrams. Do not stitch too closely as this will make the quilt feel stiff when finished. If you wish you can include floral themes or follow shapes on the printed fabrics for added interest.

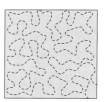

• Make it easier for yourself by handling the quilt properly. Roll up the excess quilt neatly to fit under your sewing machine arm, and use a table, or chair to help support the weight of the quilt that hangs down the other side.

Preparing to bind the edges

Once you have quilted or tied your quilt sandwich together, remove all the basting stitches. Then, baste around the outer edge of the quilt 1/4in (6mm) from the edge of the top patchwork layer. Trim the back and batting to the edge of the patchwork and straighten the edge of the patchwork if necessary.

Making the binding

1 Cut bias or straight grain strips the width required for your binding, making sure the grainline is running the correct way on your straight grain strips. Cut enough strips until you have the required length to go around the edge of your quilt.

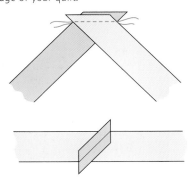

2 To join strips together, the two ends that are to be joined must be cut at a 45 degree angle, as above. Stitch right sides together, trim turnings and press seam open.

Binding the edges

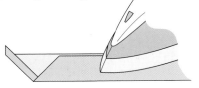

1 Cut starting end of binding strip at a 45-degree angle, fold a 1/4in (6mm) turning to wrong side along cut edge and press in place. With wrong sides together, fold strip in half lengthways, keeping raw edges level, and press.

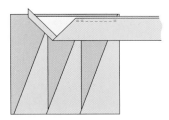

2 Starting at the centre of one of the long edges, place the doubled binding on to the right side of the quilt keeping raw edges level. Stitch the binding in place starting 1/4in (6mm) in from the diagonal folded edge (see above). Reverse stitch to secure, and working 1/4in (6mm) in from edge of the quilt towards first corner of quilt. Stop 1/4in (6mm) in from corner and work a few reverse stitches.

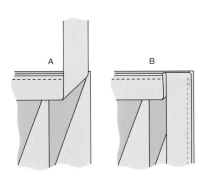

A   B

3 Fold the loose end of the binding up, making a 45-degree angle (see A). Keeping the diagonal fold in place, fold the binding back down, aligning the raw edges with the next side of the quilt. Starting at the point where the last stitch ended, stitch down the next side (see B).

4 Continue to stitch the binding in place around all the quilt edges in this way, tucking the finishing end

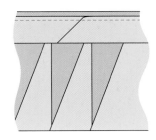

of the binding inside the diagonal starting section (see above).

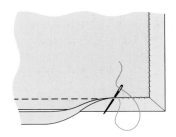

5 Turn the folded edge of the binding on to the back of the quilt. Hand stitch the folded edge in place just covering binding machine stitches, and folding a mitre at each corner.

Experience ratings

Easy, straightforward, suitable for a beginner.

Suitable for the average pachworker and quilter

For the more experienced patchworker and quilter.

All Drima and Sylko machine threads, Anchor embroidery threads, and Prym sewing aids, distributed in UK by Coats Crafts UK, P.O. Box 22, Lingfield House, Lingfield Point, McMullen Road, Darlington, Co. Durham, DL1 1YQ.

Consumer helpline: 01325 394237.

Anchor embroidery thread and Coats sewing threads, distributed in the USA by Coats & Clark,

4135 South Stream Blvd, Charlotte,

North Carolina 28217. Tel: 704 329 5016.

Fax: 704 329 5027.

Prym products distributed in the USA by Prym-Dritz Corp,

950 Brisack Road, Spartanburg, SC 29303.

Tel: +1 864 576 5050, Fax: +1 864 587 3353,

e-mail: pdmar@teleplex.net

Glossary of Terms

Appliqué The technique of stitching fabric shapes on to a background to create a design. It can be applied either by hand or machine with a decorative embroidery stitch, such as buttonhole, or satin stitch.

Backing The bottom layer of a quilt sandwich. It is made of fabric pieced to the size of the quilt top with the addition of about 3in (7.5cm) all around to allow for quilting take-up.

Basting or Tacking This is a means of holding two fabric layers or the layers of a quilt sandwich together temporarily with large hand stitches, or pins.

Batting or Wadding This is the middle layer, or padding in a quilt. It can be made of cotton, wool, silk or synthetic fibres.

Bias The diagonal grain of a fabric. This is the direction which has the most give or stretch, making it ideal for bindings, especially on curved edges.

Binding A narrow strip of fabric used to finish off the edges of quilts or projects; it can be cut on the straight grain of a fabric or on the bias.

Block A single design unit that when stitched together with other blocks create the quilt top. It is most often a square, hexagon, or rectangle, but it can be any shape. It can be pieced or plain.

Border A frame of fabric stitched to the outer edges of the quilt top. Borders can be narrow or wide, pieced or plain. As well as making the quilt larger, they unify the overall design and draw attention to the central area.

Butted corners A corner finished by stitching border strips together at right angles to each other.

Chalk pencils Available in various colours, they are used for marking lines, or spots on fabric.

Cutting mat Designed for use with a rotary cutter, it is made from a special 'self-healing' material that keeps your cutting blade sharp. Cutting mats come in various sizes and are usually marked with a grid to help you line up the edges of fabric and cut out larger pieces.

Foundation pattern A printed base exact size of a block onto which patchwork pieces are sewn. The foundations are usually made from soft paper, but could also be lightweight fabric, interfacing, or one of the new non-woven tear-away backings, such as Stitch-n-tear.

Free-motion quilting Curved wavy quilting lines stitched in a random manner. Stitching diagrams are often given for you to follow as a loose guide.

Fussy cutting This is when a template is placed on a particular motif, or stripe, to obtain interesting effects. This method is not as efficient as strip cutting, but yields very interesting results.

Grain The direction in which the threads run in a woven fabric. In a vertical direction it is called the lengthwise grain, which has very little stretch. The horizontal direction, or crosswise grain is slightly stretchy, but diagonally the fabric has a lot of stretch. This grain is called the bias. Wherever possible the grain of a fabric should run in the same direction on a quilt block and borders.

Inset seams or setting-in A patchwork technique whereby one patch (or block) is stitched into a 'V' shape formed by the joining of two other patches (or blocks).

Mitred Binding A corner finished by folding and stitching binding strips at a 45-degree angle.

Mitred Borders Borders where the corners are joined at a 45-degree angle.

Patch A small shaped piece of fabric used in the making of a patchwork pattern.

Patchwork The technique of stitching small pieces of fabric (patches) together to create a larger piece of fabric, usually forming a design.

Pieced quilt A quilt composed of patches.

Quilters' tape A narrow removable masking tape. If placed lightly on fabric, it provides a firm guideline for straight-line quilting patterns.

Quilting Traditionally done by hand with running stitches, but for speed modern quilts are often stitched by machine. The stitches are sewn through the top, wadding and backing to hold the three layers together. Quilting stitches are usually worked in some form of design, but they can be random.

Quilting hoop Consists of two wooden circular or oval rings with a screw adjuster on the outer ring. It stabilises the quilt layers, helping to create an even tension.

Quilt sandwich Three layers of fabric: a decorative top, wadding and backing held together with quilting stitches.

Rotary cutter A sharp circular blade attached to a handle for quick, accurate cutting. It is a device that can be used to cut up to six layers of fabric at one time. It must be used in conjunction with a 'self-healing' cutting mat and a thick plastic ruler.

Rotary ruler A thick, clear plastic ruler printed with lines that are exactly _in (6mm) apart. Sometimes they also have diagonal lines printed on, indicating 45 and 60-degree angles. A rotary ruler is used as a guide when cutting out fabric pieces using a rotary cutter.

Sashing A piece or pieced sections of fabric interspaced between blocks.

Sashing Posts When blocks have sashing between them the corner squares are known as sashing posts.

Selvedges Also known as selvages, these are the firmly woven edges down each side of a fabric length. Selvedges should be trimmed off before cutting out your fabric, as they are more liable to shrink when the fabric is washed.

Stitch-in-the-ditch or Ditch quilting Also known as quilting-in-the-ditch. The quilting stitches are worked along the actual seam lines, to give a pieced quilt texture.

Suffolk Puffs or Yo-Yos A circle of fabric double the size of the finished puff is gathered up into a rosette shape.

Template A pattern piece used as a guide for marking and cutting out fabric patches, or marking a quilting, or appliqué design. Usually made from plastic or strong card that can be reused many times.

Threads One hundred percent cotton or cotton-covered polyester is best for hand and machine piecing. Choose a colour that matches your fabric. When sewing different colours and patterns together, choose a medium to light neutral colour, such as grey or ecru. Specialist quilting threads are available for hand and machine quilting.

Walking foot or Quilting foot This is a sewing machine foot with dual feed control. It is very helpful when quilting, as the fabric layers are fed evenly from the top and below, reducing the risk of slippage and puckering.

The Kaffe Fassett Fabric Collection

Shot Cotton

SC 01 Ginger   SC 02 Cassis   SC 03 Prune   SC 04 Slate   SC 05 Opal   SC 07 Persimmon

SC 08 Raspberry   SC 09 Pomegranate   SC 10 Bittersweet   SC 11 Tangerine   SC 12 Chartreuse   SC 14 Lavender

SC 15 Denim Blue   SC 16 Mustard   SC 17 Sage   SC 18 Tobacco   SC 19 Lichen   SC 20 Smoky

SC 21 Pine   SC 22 Pewter   SC 23 Stone Grey   SC 24 Ecru   SC 25 Charcoal   SC 26 Duck Egg

SC 27 Grass   SC 28 Blush   SC 31 Mushroom   SC 32 Rosy   SC 33 Water Melon   SC 34 Lemon

SC 35 Sunshine   SC 36 Lilac   SC 37 Coffee   SC 38 Biscuit   SC 39 Apple   SC 40 Cobalt

SC 41 Jade   SC 42 Rush   SC 43 Lime   SC 44 Scarlet   SC 45 True Cobalt   SC 46 Aegean

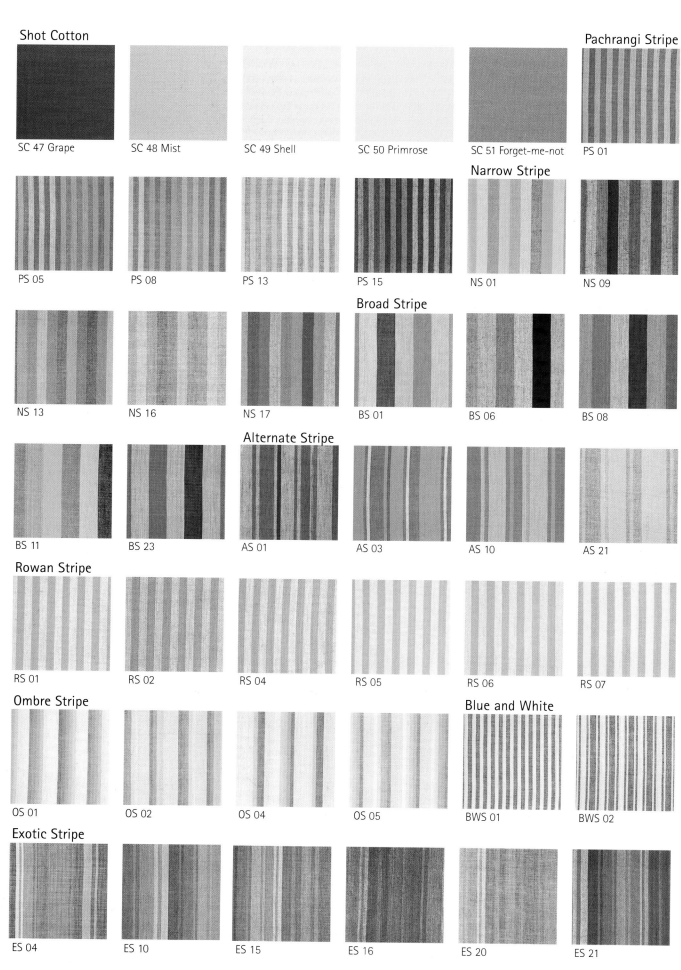

Shot Cotton

SC 47 Grape

SC 48 Mist

SC 49 Shell

SC 50 Primrose

SC 51 Forget-me-not

Pachrangi Stripe

PS 01

PS 05

PS 08

PS 13

PS 15

Narrow Stripe

NS 01

NS 09

NS 13

NS 16

NS 17

Broad Stripe

BS 01

BS 06

BS 08

BS 11

BS 23

Alternate Stripe

AS 01

AS 03

AS 10

AS 21

Rowan Stripe

RS 01

RS 02

RS 04

RS 05

RS 06

RS 07

Ombre Stripe

OS 01

OS 02

OS 04

OS 05

Blue and White

BWS 01

BWS 02

Exotic Stripe

ES 04

ES 10

ES 15

ES 16

ES 20

ES 21

Broad Check

BC 04

BC 02

BC 03

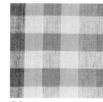

BC 01

Exotic Check

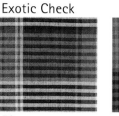

EC 01

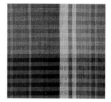

EC 05

Narrow Check

NC 01

NC 02

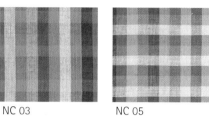

NC 03

NC 05

Single Ikat Wash

SIW 01 Peach

SIW 02 Blue

SIW 03 Banana

SIW 04 Green

SIW 05 Lavender

SIW 06 Red

Double Ikat Checkerboard

DIC 01 Scarlet

DIC 02 Magenta

DIC 03 Indigo

DIC 04 Gold

DIC 05 Swede

DIC 06 Blue

Double Ikat Polka

DIP 01 Sage

DIP 02 Pumpkin

DIP 03 Scarlet

DIP 04 Denim

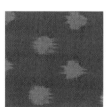

DIP 05 Blue

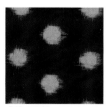

DIP 06 Navy

Roman Glass

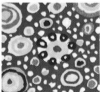

GP01-BW

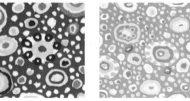

GP01-C

GP01-G

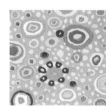

GP01-J

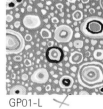

GP01-L

GP01-P

Chard

GP01-PK

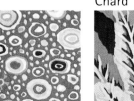

GP01-R

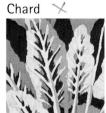

GP01-S

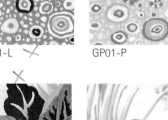

GP09-J

GP09-L

GP09-P

Damask

GP 02-J

GP 02-L

GP 02-P

GP 02-SM

GP 02-PG

GP 02-SA

Artichokes

Peony

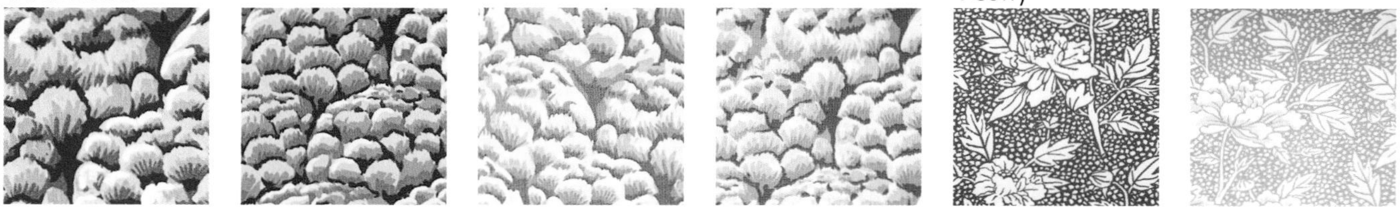

GP 07-C

GP 07-J

GP 07-L

GP 07-P

GP 17-BL

GP 17-GR

GP 17-OC

GP 17-TA

GP 17-VI

GP 17-GN

GP 17-MR

GP 17-RD

Fruit Basket

GP 19-RD

GP 19-AP

GP 19-PK

GP 19-BL

GP 19-BK

GP 19-TE

Gazania

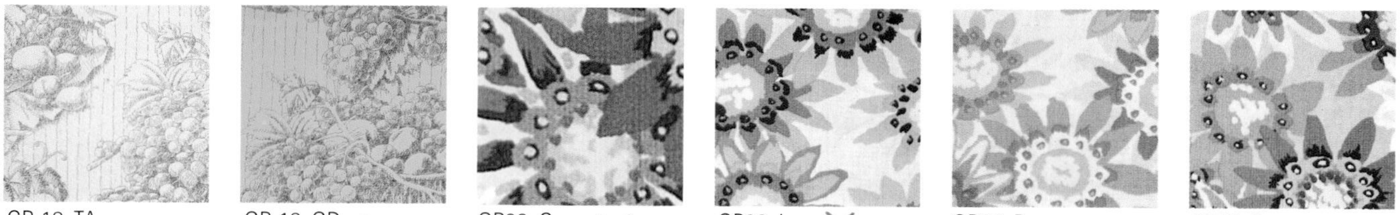

GP 19-TA

GP 19-GD

GP03-C

GP03-L

GP03-P

GP03-S

Dotty

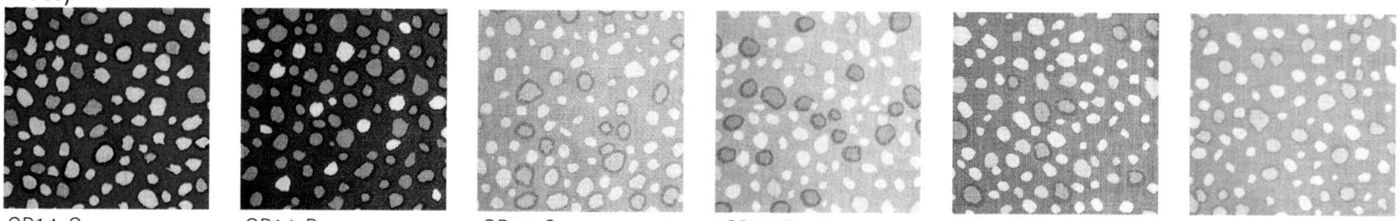

GP14-C

GP14-P

GP14-O

GP14-T

GP14-D

GP14-SG

Bubbles

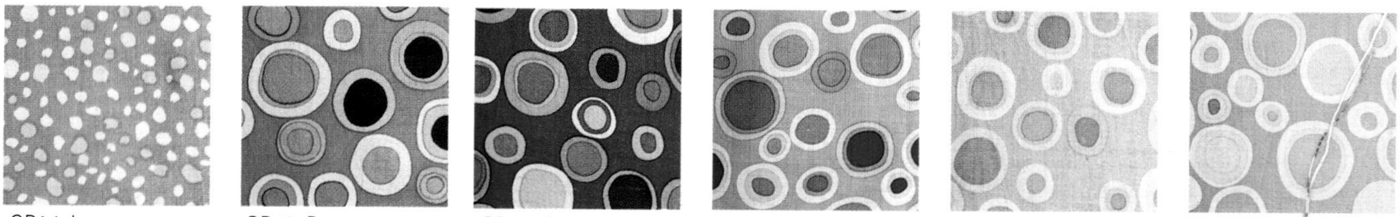

GP14-L

GP15-P

GP15-C

GP15-S

GP15-G

GP15-O

Mosaic

GP16-PU

GP16-RG

GP16-PK

GP16-BL

GP16-GR

August Roses

GP18-PU

GP18-OC

GP18-MG

GP18-PK

GP18-PT

Forget-Me-Not Roses

GP08-MG

GP08-BW

GP08-L

GP08-J

GP08-C

Chrysanthemum

GP13-B

GP13-R

GP13-GN

GP13-O

GP13-GR

Floral Dance

GP12-MG

GP12-B

GP12-P

GP12-O

GP12-MV

Paperweight

GP20-CB

GP20-SL

GP20-LM

GP20-PN

GP20-PT

Pansy

GP23-GY

GP23-MT

GP23-BL

GP23-GD

GP23-BR

100% Cotton
Fabric width 45ins (114cm)
Wash fabric before use

Diagonal Poppy

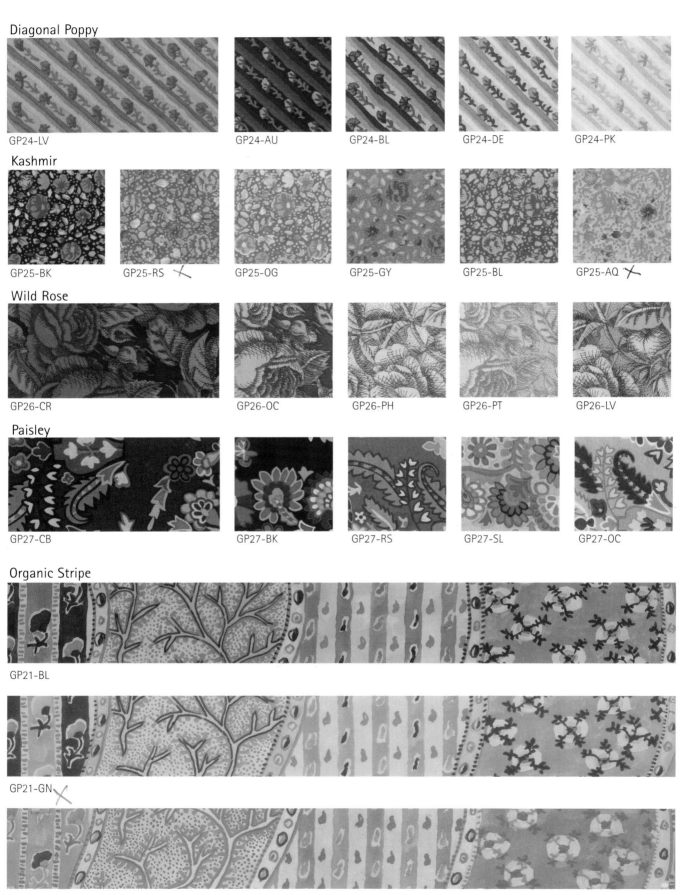

GP24-LV GP24-AU GP24-BL GP24-DE GP24-PK

Kashmir

GP25-BK GP25-RS GP25-OG GP25-GY GP25-BL GP25-AQ

Wild Rose

GP26-CR GP26-OC GP26-PH GP26-PT GP26-LV

Paisley

GP27-CB GP27-BK GP27-RS GP27-SL GP27-OC

Organic Stripe

GP21-BL

GP21-GN

GP21-PK

Please note:
The fabric swatches (shown on these pages) are not accurate in scale. To check
the scale please refer to the patchwork images at the front of the book.

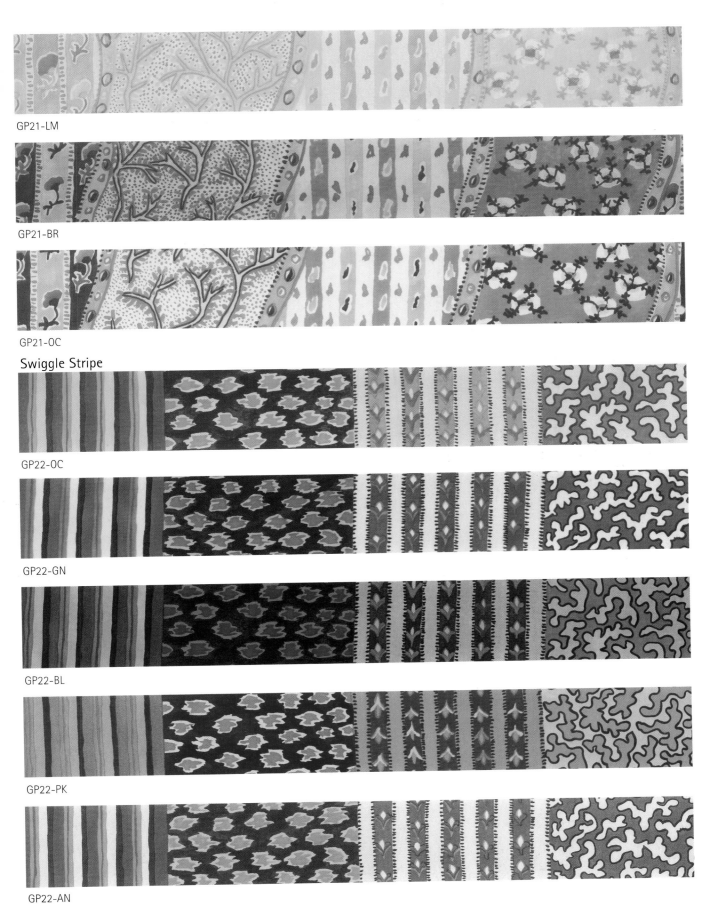

GP21-LM

GP21-BR

GP21-OC

Swiggle Stripe

GP22-OC

GP22-GN

GP22-BL

GP22-PK

GP22-AN

Biographies

Sandy Donabed

"The fabric is generally the focus of my work. I usually start with a piece that speaks to me and take off from there- the stories develop in my subconscious as I work. In fact, when I finish a piece I rarely remember the process of making it but I do know the associations and the stories that give it meaning. My newer work has focused on exploring collage techniques, and these seem to be done as a result of a need to layer and add images on top of images. All my work has a back-story, a meaning, and I never just focus on line or color for it's own sake. I have gotten further and further from traditional quilt making, but I just cannot give up that final split from working with layers and stitchery. I hope I never do."

Roberta Horton

Roberta Horton of Berkeley, California has been a quiltmaker for over 30 years. She has taught and lectured worldwide. Her study and love of quilts has pushed her into developing many workshops and to the authoring of six books. Roberta was the recipient of the 2000 Silver Star Award presented by the International Quilt Assosiation. This was in recognition of her lifetime body of work and the long-term effect it has had on quilting.

Brandon Mably

A regular contributor to the Rowan Patchwork books Brandon Mably has built a reputation as a quilt designer of simple, elegant quilts in restful colours. Brandon trained at The Kaffe Fassett Studio. He designs for the Rowan and Vogue Knitting magazine knitwear collections, and is the author of 'Brilliant Knits'.

Mary Mashuta

California quiltmaker Mary Mashuta has been making quilts and wearables for over thirty yea She is a professionally trained teacher who has been teaching internationally since 1985. Her classes always stress easily understood colour and design. S knows that no quilter can own t much fabric, and she enjoys discovering new blocks to showcase personal collections.

y Mennesson

Liza Prior Lucy

Pauline Smith

Gill Turley

began quilting and working
fabric in the late 90's. She
d that piecing the quilt
ne the foundation of the
ct and that the free motion
ng made the design come
The movement within Kaffe's
s really inspired her free
on quilting. She particularly
using the solid shot cottons
Kaffe's collections as backing,
nly do the quilting designs
pop but it is like quilting
gh butter. Betsy lives just a
miles outside of Sisters,
on, home of the Stitchin' Post
he Sisters Outdoor Quilt
. She has worked for and
inspired by the owner Jean
and her daughter Valori and
ontributed quilts to a number
eir books.

Liza Prior Lucy first began making
quilts in 1990. She was so
enthralled by the craftspeople she
met and by the generously stocked
quilt fabric shops in the States that
quiltmaking soon became a
passion. Liza originally trained as a
knitwear designer and produced
features for needlework magazines.
She also owned and operated her
own needlepoint shop in
Washington, D.C. Liza met Kaffe
when she was working as a sales
representative for Rowan Yarns in
the New York City area - Kaffe had
come to America to promote his
books and was working as Rowan's
leading designer. They worked
closely together in the States and
the UK to write and produce the
quilts for the books Glorious
Patchwork and Passionate
Patchwork.

Pauline Smith has been a quilt
maker since a college visit to The
American Museum in Bath in 1968.
With a successful business
designing, making and selling
patchwork through exhibition and
commissions she has been involved
in the development of patchwork
at Rowan since 1998. Pauline
designs by playing with the fabrics
until she is happy with how they
work together. During this process
ideas for the quilt design emerge.
As the Rowan patchwork co-
ordinator, she works closely with
Kaffe Fassett and everyone
involved in producing the
'Patchwork and Quilting' series.

Gill is a well-established British
Quilter, best known for her country
quilts and her great passion for
simple quilts from the past. She is
an experienced tutor having taught
and lectured in many parts of the
U.K. and mainland Europe. Prior to
working on Rowan Patchwork and
Quilting Book Number 6, Gill has
contributed to a number of recent
quilt books and international
magazines.

Other ROWAN Titles Available

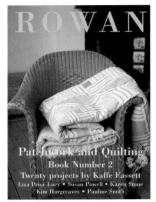

Patchwork and Quilting
Book Number Two
£9.95

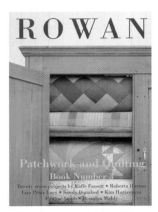

Patchwork and Quilting
Book Number Three
£10.95

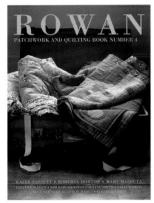

Patchwork and Quilting
Book Number Four
£12.95

Patchwork and Quilting
Book Number Five
£13.95

Seven Easy Pieces
£7.95

Rowan Living
Book One
£12.95

Rowan Creative Living
Book Two
£12.95

R O W A N

Green Lane Mill, Holmfirth, West Yorkshire, England
Tel: +44 (0) 1484 681881   Fax: +44 (0) 1484 687920   Internet: www.knitrowan.com
Email: mail@knitrowan.com